MISSING LINKS

Building truly interconnected organisations delivers better results

Phil Abbott and Paul Fellows

ARCH – Achieving Real Change

Copyright© 2012 Phil Abbott & Paul Fellows

Phil Abbott & Paul Fellows have asserted the right to be identified as the authors of the work in accordance with the Copyright, Designs and Patents Act 1988.

First published in Great Britain in 2012
ARCH – Achieving Real Change
38 Muir Drive
Hingham
Norwich
NR9 4PQ
United Kingdom

All rights reserved. Except for the quotation of short passages for the purposes of criticism and review, no part of this publication may be reproduced, stored in a retrieval system, or transmitted in any form or by any means, electronic, mechanical, photocopying, recording or otherwise, without the prior written permission of the publishers.

A CIP catalogue record is available from the British Library.

ISBN 978-0-9571288-0-4

Printed and bound in the UK by Davis, Simpson & Davis Limited, 13a St. James Street, Kings Lynn, Norfolk PE30 5DA

Missing Links is dedicated to all those individuals who are striving to ensure their organisations work in the most effective manner, and who may not always be listened to or recognised.

To Maureen

With grateful thanks for many years of comradeship, and help with this book.

Introduction

Chapter 1 What is the problem?
Many organisations do not work as a single integrated whole and as a result do not achieve their full potential.

Chapter 2 Myths and mistaken beliefs
A number of key things that are assumed to help organisations perform also prevent the fulfilment of their true bottom-line potential.

Chapter 3 Why our holistic approach?
Our holistic approach gets to the heart of the matter. It gets people into a state of mind where they think of the implications for the whole organisation of what they are doing.

Chapter 4 The self-aware CEO
How you as the CEO carry out your role has a major impact on organisational performance in ways you may not realise.

Chapter 5 Everyone owns the bottom-line
In a cohesive organisation everyone's' efforts are aligned to achieving the same business result.

Chapter 6 Engaged with customers
The success of your organisation depends on your customers. The closer you engage with them the more likely you are to succeed.

Chapter 7 Understanding Individuals
Every person in the organisation brings a distinct collection of skills, qualities and attributes. Making the best use of these will help to fulfil the organisation's potential.

Chapter 8 Genuine teamwork
Understanding each collection of individuals and how they relate to other collections provides genuine solutions that improve cohesion and performance.

Chapter 9 Mutually understood communications
Genuine two way communication does not happen naturally. It needs to be worked on in the right way.

Chapter 10 Shepherding organisational culture
To maximise bottom-line results organisation culture must be guided to ensure that 'the way we do things round here' is what you want to happen.

Chapter 11 User useful systems
In a cohesive organisation IT must be tuned to the needs of the business and of the people who use it. This requires genuine teamwork between users and IT professionals.

Chapter 12 Restructuring delivers the goods

More than half of mergers and acquisitions fail to deliver their stated value and many restructuring exercises are carried out for a hidden agenda. However, in a cohesive organisation, far-reaching changes such as these are carried out thoroughly and deliver the vast majority of their stated aims.

Chapter 13 Cohesive Public Services

Public sector organisations differ in certain ways from private sector ones. However they share many of the same issues. This chapter identifies differences and outlines how they relate to our holistic model.

Chapter 14 How you do it

If you wish to improve the cohesiveness of your organisation this chapter outlines how you might do it.

Missing Links Executive Summary

Author Profiles

Introduction

Throughout both of our careers we have sought individually and collectively to improve bottom-line results. We have focused on developing both sustainable businesses and profits in the private sector, and effective public services, which meet people's needs, in the public sector.

We have always looked at the wider picture not just to try and solve the immediate problem. Everything happens within a context and this context can change. Sustained performance in the longer run requires the ever changing mix of internal and external factors to be dealt with together as a single whole.

This book has its roots in Eastern Europe where we first came together. The more we talked, the more we found we were both endeavouring to do the same thing. Our focus on what to do with organisations to achieve the best effect was in complete alignment. We both had many elements of the jig-saw which enables this to happen, but it was only when we put them together that we were able to produce a comprehensive picture of what is required.

Why hasn't this been written about before? There are many excellent works dealing with aspects of what organisations need to do, and some which deal with the organisation as a single entity. However none that we have found link all the necessary elements together into a single whole in such a way that the underlying mechanisms are also dealt with.

Things happen for a reason. Sometimes the wrong things happen despite everyone's best intentions and efforts. So we have endeavoured to describe in this book not just what it is organisations need to do to survive and thrive, but also why this is the case.

We trust you will enjoy reading it. We hope it will cause you not only to think about the organisation you are in charge of or make a contribution to, but also to take informed action to improve those all-important bottom-line results.

We would like to thank the many colleagues we have worked with who have contributed in some way to the contents of the book. Specifically our thanks go to Dr. Maureen Gardiner and Alex Abbott for their assistance in reviewing the contents, not to mention our respective families and friends for their support.

Chapter 1 - What is the problem?

The Issue

Why have we written this book? What is the problem we are trying to help people understand and fix?

What is the problem?

We have frequently observed that organisations do not work together as a single integrated whole. As a result they fail to fully maximise their potential and end up producing lower profits and inferior results than they should be achieving.

What people typically say

- "The left hand doesn't know what the right hand is doing; sometimes it doesn't even know what it is doing itself!" - said by customers and staff.
- "Managers don't know what really goes on at the front-line" - said by the staff.
- "The CEO is responsible for the way the organisation operates."- said by the staff and often the managers.
- "Why don't people do what I tell them?" - said by the CEO.
- "I get my job done, it's up to everyone else to get their own jobs done" - said by middle managers.
- "We don't take any notice of what they say – they don't know what they are talking about" - said by staff in one section about staff in another.
- "If only they'd listen to us we wouldn't be in the mess we are" - said by specialists whose input has been ignored.

What can we deduce from this?

In many instances no-one is responsible for ensuring that the various parts of the organisation work together. Even the CEO does not always feel able to make it happen. People seem more comfortable staying within their own area and keeping their head down

Chapter 1 - What is the problem?

and doing what is immediately in front of them. Small wonder then that the following things can easily happen:

- Products are designed which can't be made effectively or at the right price.
- Sales staff make promises which can't be delivered.
- Deadlines and targets are set which can't be met.
- Systems are produced which don't meet operational needs.
- New ways of working are introduced without fully assessing their impact.

A picture paints a thousand words. Here is one which illustrates the lack of cohesion that can occur in organisations. You may have seen it before:

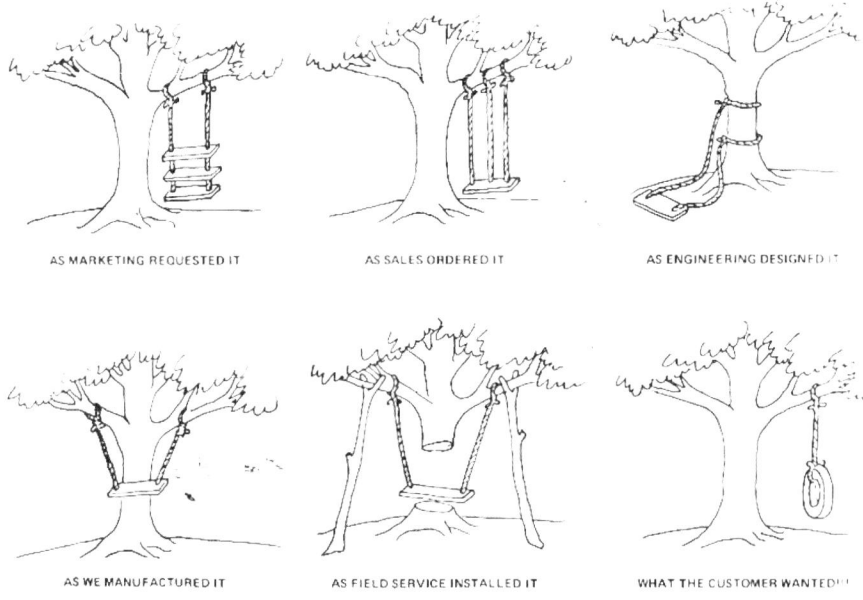

This shows what can happen in an extreme case. People have pursued their own ideas, failed to talk to each other and not cooperated. They have remained in their own silos. It is

Chapter 1 - What is the problem?

typical for people to see the part of the organisation they work in as distinct and separate from others. They understand it best. They don't know as much about all the other parts. They don't know how to interact with them. Failure to work together costs you money.

What is required?

People need to work together so that their organisation achieves a state of cohesion. People's efforts should be aligned towards meeting the organisation's objectives so that they interact with one another in a positive and constructive way.

Why doesn't it happen?

You may ask why this doesn't happen as a matter of course. In our view it is because of one or all of the following reasons:

- No-one believes they have the authority to do it.
- If someone has the authority they don't have the tools at their disposal.
- There is no common understanding of how to achieve cohesion.
- People are not interested in it because they don't believe that it is their job to do it.
- People feel safer staying in their own 'silo'.

What are the consequences?

Failure to align people's efforts with the organisation can in extreme situations have catastrophic consequences.

The collapse of the banking sector in recent years happened because people made short term decisions rather than considering the long term effects. Products were designed which someone in management thought were viable agreed to sign off. However there were insufficient links with other arms of the organisation such as risk management and economists. It is clear in retrospect that certain members of staff pointed out the dangers. They were not only not listened to, but in some banks, staff who challenged the wisdom of

Chapter 1 - What is the problem?

what was happening were dismissed because they were not following the management line. The inevitable result of not working together was that some banks failed to survive. Others ended up being rescued by taxpayers.

Fortunately such an acute crisis doesn't, of course, happen in all organisations. Yet many suffer from chronic under-performance. Too many settle for 'business as usual' as they feel unable, or in some cases unwilling, to do better. In doing this they lose opportunities, waste resources and ultimately pay for it on the bottom-line.

Any organisation has beliefs about itself which justify the way it operates. Many of the most common ones are incorrect. This means that the organisation (and the people in it) is deluding itself. Small delusions are harmless; big ones can wreck the company. We have spent many years observing these in operation. The next Chapter explores what we have found.

Chapter 2 - Myths and Mistaken Beliefs

The issue

Organisations often function around a number of what we call 'myths'. These myths are assumptions about how things work which provide guidance, consistency and much comfort to many. They are neither positive nor negative but are descriptions of how things are. Because they are accepted as such they can lead to consequent mistaken beliefs which in large measure can cause problems and difficulties.

These myths help people to understand what to do and what not to do. But from these also flow the mistaken beliefs that may be counter-productive and get in the way of the bottom-line. So myths are double-edged in nature. They bring problems as well as benefits. The consequence is that they lead to attitudes and behaviours which detract from cohesive effort within organisations.

You may recognise many of the statements we have included in this Chapter. You may also say that they don't all apply in your organisation or that there are others you have observed. What follows is meant to be indicative not comprehensive. It is designed to help you think through and question what may be happening in your own organisation.

Myth - the division of labour enables business to function

All businesses and organisations function on the basis that the work carried out is divided amongst the employees in such a way that each individual or group of individuals knows what they are concentrating on. This means that work is allocated to people who are qualified and skilled enough to do it. By each person concentrating on a particular set of responsibilities they are able to build up experience and to perform more efficiently. For this to work well in reality a number of conditions need to be met.

- Each person understands what their contribution is supposed to be.
- Each part of the organisation will communicate with the other parts it needs to connect with.
- Everybody is on the same page.
- Everybody is willing to cooperate with others.
- If people are moved around it is done in a deliberate and organised fashion.

Chapter 2 - Myths and Mistaken Beliefs

It can be a mistaken belief that having divided work up into separate components conditions will automatically occur that allow cohesive operations to happen. The fundamental mistaken belief is that everyone collaborates within an organisation. In fact antagonisms often exist that prevent it from happening. These can be between individuals, groups of individuals or whole departments.

Myth - size is a measure of success

Most commentaries on what is happening in the business market place base their assumptions on the premise that bigger organisations are in most instances better than smaller ones. The accent is on growth, economies of scale and elimination of competition by acquisition. Staying the same size or reducing in size is viewed as a lack of success.

The types of potentially mistaken beliefs that this can lead to include:

- Anything which generates growth is good.
- Achievement must be in numbers to have meaning.
- What counts are hard measures.
- Mergers and acquisitions increase value.
- We are OK because we are bigger than everyone else.

Size is often used to increase people's status. It makes the senior executives feel more important because they are in charge of something bigger whilst also carrying the assumption that the organisation is more robust. There are many corporate examples of business failure in large organisations which illustrates that size is not necessarily a guarantor of success. It is often the case that smaller units within large conglomerates are the most profitable.

Myth - successful CEOs are omnipotent

In the world we live in, significant emphasis is placed on the influence of leaders in determining outcomes. There is often an innate assumption that to change an ailing company, government or sporting team it is necessary is to change the person at the head of the organisation for all to be well again. It is as if everything can be solved by this single act. This can lead to mistaken beliefs in the organisation which support this myth such as:

Chapter 2 - Myths and Mistaken Beliefs

- I make the decisions and therefore it will happen in the way I expect it to.

- My people will tell me everything so I can make the right decisions.

- As I am in charge I can choose to ignore the rules if I want to.

- The employees believe the MD will solve everything.

- What I think happens, happens.

The danger is that everyone in an organisation may use the concept of omnipotent CEOs as an excuse for not doing what they should be doing. This means that they don't take decisions or use their initiative. Hence in their minds they cannot be blamed. All of which slows down operations and performance suffers as a result.

Myth - experts know best

As we increasingly know more and more about less and less the role of the expert, as opposed to the generalist, has become more prominent. There is a ready acceptance that people with qualifications and recognition from professional colleagues are in the best position to deal with difficult and complex issues within their areas of expertise. The mistaken beliefs that can arise from this myth are:

- We are the specialists on this subject in our organisations so we know best.

- I have read the books and gained the qualification so I know how to do it.

- Experience can be equated with expertise.

- The only people capable of commenting on this are the experts.

- The ordinary person has nothing worthwhile to contribute.

- You haven't the qualification needed to comment.

Over reliance on experts leads to an inability of the organisation to act on its own or to place too much of the burden on a small number of specific individuals. It also carries the implication that the opinions of everyone else (i.e. the non-experts) are of no value. The people carrying out a job always know what is good and bad about it. They may not have the wider picture but they do understand their part of it.

Chapter 2 - Myths and Mistaken Beliefs

Myth - organisations know what customers want

Every business or organisation has to have a product or service that it supplies. The way in which these are designed and developed is determined by the organisations that produce them. The assumption always is that they are what the customer wants and that they will sell whether they have been based on market research or not. The mistaken beliefs that can arise from this myth are:

- Our customers are loyal.
- We value all our customers.
- We are what we say we are.
- We know better than our customers what they want.
- Customers recognise the value of our products.
- If we actively promote our products customers will want more of them.
- How and where we organise customer services is not a significant issue for our customers.

Only customers themselves really know whether they are satisfied with what you are providing. Just because the organisations thinks it is wonderful doesn't mean that it is.

Myth - businesses focus on the essential things they need to do

There is a tacit assumption that all organisations do what they need to do to satisfy their stakeholders to the exclusion of everything else. They are doing what they are supposed to be doing and not wasting effort and resources on non-essential activities. The mistaken beliefs that can arise from this myth are:

- The needs and priorities of management are subordinated to those of the shareholders and the customers.
- Outsourcing non-essential operations has no effect on the workings of the rest of the business.
- Everything we do is essential.

Chapter 2 - Myths and Mistaken Beliefs

- All our decisions have the best interest of the business in mind.

The tendency is for all of us to look at things from our own individual perspective. This makes it hard to take account of the fact that other people see things differently and that they may be right.

Myth - certain types of people suit certain types of organisation best

The best benchmark comparison that people have for assessing others is themselves. If they get someone with similar beliefs, perspectives and ways of doing things they will be comfortable with them and tend to value them highly. They will often be less comfortable with people with obviously different personal approaches, ways of looking at things and working practices. Organisations naturally collect people with similarities because they fit in more easily than people with differences. The mistaken beliefs that can arise from this myth are:

- Everyone who is like me will be good at their job because I am good at mine.
- I know what is good for people because I know what is good for me.
- If I know it's right everyone else will see that it is right.
- You can't go wrong if you follow my example.
- It is easier for people who are similar to work together.
- You need to be this kind of person to fit in here.

People come in all kinds of shapes and sizes. If everyone is the same they will make similar contributions. To succeed organisations need a variety of people with diverse approaches to fit with the variety of circumstances they will encounter.

Summary

To sum up, the myths that help organisations to perform can also lead to mistaken beliefs that get in the way of performance improvement. The positive things you do can also have unforeseen negative consequences. The challenge is often to prevent your greatest strengths from becoming your greatest weaknesses.

Chapter 2 - Myths and Mistaken Beliefs

In the next chapter we move on to discuss a holistic approach that deals with these myths and mistaken beliefs and provides you with a framework to address them.

Chapter 3 - Why our holistic approach?

The issue

A means is needed that adds to conventional thinking and enables the myths and mistaken beliefs to be dealt with alongside other organisational issues. This chapter provides an outline of our distinctive approach. It has been developed from understanding why things happen and how they need to fit together.

What is our holistic approach?

For the sake of clarity 'holistic' means:

> "Dealing with or treating the whole of something or someone and not just a part" (Cambridge Dictionary Online).

Our holistic approach gets to the heart of the matter. It gets people into a state of mind where they think of the implications for the whole organisation of what they are doing. It recognises that everything that happens has consequences - some may be intentional, some unintentional. Your bottom-line result is a consequence of how you apply the whole efforts of the organisation. The more cohesive they are, the less wasted energy and the better the outcome.

This happens because all aspects of an organisation are interlinked. The degree to which these links work effectively determines how good the bottom-line performance is. To achieve lasting improvements to your bottom-line you need to develop a state of mind that looks at the organisation as a whole and have a clear understanding of how things fit together. You must look at everything and exclude nothing. We will amplify what constitutes this state of mind as we examine each of the above mentioned aspects in the chapters which follow this one.

What goes wrong - why?

Problem solving in organisations frequently focuses on what has gone wrong. There are reasons why this happens:

Chapter 3 - Why our holistic approach?

- When something goes wrong, and the pressure is on to fix it, the natural reaction is to deal with it without as a matter of course tracing the cause. This solves a problem but not necessarily the whole problem or the right problem.
- People tend to deal with what is within their span of control and to avoid, or to feel uncomfortable, involving people from other areas.
- Problems get neatly compartmentalised as this approach fits within the concept of the division of responsibilities. It is also a way of confining the problem. However the real problem may actually cross organisational boundaries.
- Investigating further may cause 'turf' disputes or require dealing with managers and staff in other areas.

The focus on what has gone wrong fits in with a model of management that has a 'telling' approach and hierarchical structure. Easy to understand, easy to control, provides an apparent degree of clarity.

However it is vital not just to focus on the 'what' but also to find out 'why' something has happened. In the real world organisations do not function in the same way as organisation charts draw them. They are not a neat pyramid - this only happens on paper. By accurately assessing the 'why' you can ensure that corrective action is applied where it works effectively, so that it will continue to solve the problems identified. This is because almost every aspect of an organisation has an impact on almost every other one within its operations. If you look at and understand it as a complete whole with the links between each part, you will identify the real problems and apply the real solutions. If you look at each aspect in isolation you may end up in optimising one aspect whilst potentially exacerbating other aspects that are inextricably linked to it.

Holistic Diagram

The purpose of the following diagram is to help people understand what they have possibly been missing before. It describes the key elements of the state of mind you need to have to fully appreciate the organisation and where it needs to head. It is not a model (in the strictest sense of the word) and it is not a product. It is how you look at things and approach changes.

Chapter 3 - Why our holistic approach?

In examining it the reader will notice that it does not mention functional parts of the organisation. This is not to say that they are not important. This is because the diagram is not an organisation chart but a way of looking at how underlying aspects of an organisation inter-relate. Our working assumption is that if a function is present in an organisation it is needed in order to achieve the required business results.

Taking each of these aspects in turn:

Self-aware CEO

CEOs have a major impact on their organisations. Often this can be far beyond and different to what they think it is. They may assume that they are having a particular effect

Chapter 3 - Why our holistic approach?

when in fact the effect is somewhat different. Others may well be aware of this but are too frightened to tell the CEO. Therefore in order to manage the resultant consequences of their approach, the CEO needs to be sufficiently self-aware about what they themselves are doing and why they are doing it.

Everyone owns the bottom-line

If people throughout an organisation understand and feel a sense of ownership of the bottom-line, they will align their activities towards optimising it, as opposed to abdicating responsibility for it.

Engage with customers

Customers pay money to the organisation for their products and/or services. If there are no customers the organisation goes out of business. Positively engaging with them should be the norm, as opposed to a veneer of customer service being used as a smokescreen for the business doing what it likes.

Understanding individuals

The only active ingredient in an organisation is its people. To gain the most from them they need to be understood as individuals for the skills and attributes they bring. Not as mere units of human resource who are treated as all the same.

Genuine teamwork

Much use is made of the word 'teamwork'. Effective teamwork only happens when those involved are genuine in their commitment and their actions. Otherwise it is always someone else's fault. Part of this inter-team work is about jointly addressing issues and acknowledging each team's requirements and behaviour, not blaming the other team for what is going wrong.

Chapter 3 - Why our holistic approach?

Mutually understood communications

Communication is a two way process. Without mutual understanding the messages sent out are incorrectly received and hence responded to inappropriately. Telling is not communicating. Interaction is required for mutual understanding to occur.

Shepherding organisational culture

Every organisation has a 'way we do things round here'. This happens whether there are instructions or not. It is a behavioural pattern that is adopted as opposed to being directed by management. It needs to be attuned to achieving the organisation's desired results. To do so requires involvement not instruction.

User useful systems

Systems, whether manual or technological, are a means to an end, not an end in themselves. Effective systems are useful to those that use them because they enable the required results to be delivered. Systems don't create themselves, people design them. If a system does not meet the needs of its intended users it is because all those involved with designing it didn't do their job well enough.

Restructuring delivers the goods

Too often restructuring exercises are embarked upon to deal with problems that management could have solved anyway. In an ideal organisation restructurings will deliver the benefits they were intended to produce. The same applies to mergers and acquisitions. They should improve the position, outlook, performance and value of the whole aggregate organisation. If they don't why undertake them?

Summary

The long term success of an organisation is centred on its ability to move in a controlled and effective manner from where it is to where it wants to be. It must focus and coordinate the energy of its actions and its people towards this goal in steps of a manageable size.

Chapter 3 - Why our holistic approach?

This may seem like common sense. It therefore begs the question - if the route to success is so self-evident why do so many organisations fail to achieve it? Following our holistic approach outlined above enables this achievement to take place.

What follows is a more detailed look at each of the elements of our holistic approach. This includes many working examples both of what can go wrong and how to do it right to create greater cohesion in your organisation. Such cohesion will have a positive impact on your bottom-line results.

Chapter 4 - The self-aware CEO

The issue

The CEO (Chief Executive Officer) has a connection to everything and an influence on all things.

All CEOs know what the above diagram shows - that because they are CEOs they are inextricably linked to all aspects of the organisation. What we have found is that they often don't understand their impact and why things don't happen as they expect them to.

This chapter examines ways in which a CEO can be self-aware in order to be able to develop a state of mind that promotes a holistic view of the organisation.

Chapter 4 - The self-aware CEO

Role of the CEO

You will recall in Chapter 2 that we said one of the myths in organisations is that 'successful MDs are omnipotent'. In our view the role of the successful, bottom-line leader is not to be a dictator isolated from the rest of the team but to be a person who works with his or her people to ensure that the elements of the business perform properly together. This is based on our observation that successful organisations are complex inter-connected networks of people and actions working together effectively to generate the best products and services and to produce optimum profit.

In these organisations the CEO is a facilitator as well as a decision maker. He or she must know what is going on, be aware of critical issues and be able to take informed decisions. They should be seen as part of the team not an Inquisitor sitting in judgement above all others. They should be part of the business, not separated from it and should be skilled in balancing the attention they pay to internal and external issues. Sometimes it is too easy for someone at the head of a business to forget what happens 'further down the line' in an organisation. Approaching things in this way may be critical in determining whether it is success or failure that results.

The CEO is at the centre of an inter-connected web that forms the structure of every enterprise. No two CEOs are alike, just as no two organisations are. What works in one place will not necessarily work in another. We have however observed that successful CEOs are skilled in connecting people and activities in ways that best achieve bottom-line success and add lasting value. They are also very proficient at identifying and listening to the relevant and honest messages from their people.

The Style and Approach of the CEO

Each CEO has their own individual personal style and approach. This is an integral part of you as a person. It consists of your way of thinking, your way of behaving, your personal characteristics, attitudes, beliefs and motivation. Collectively these constitute what you are, and what you are gives rise to your impact on the organisation. Much of what you are you take for granted because you live with it day in, day out. What you may not fully appreciate

Chapter 4 - The self-aware CEO

is how different that is to how other people are and what things are made easier or more difficult as a consequence.

> Example 1 – Impact of CEO's Style
>
> A major European business had a very charismatic President. He believed that he communicated clearly and that people knew what was going on. Unfortunately he did not fully understand the personal styles and approaches of his Head Office managers. They felt uncomfortable about questioning or discussing ideas with him. Instead they had a tendency to interpret what he said by 'reading between the lines'. On his visits to subsidiaries in various parts of the world the President was surprised to discover some of the actions being implemented. He was even more surprised to be told that they were being done because they had been told that it was what he wanted.

You need to be fully aware of the whole of your personality as this forms the bedrock to everything you do. If you haven't had this analysed you should. If you have, you should check with an appropriate specialist your understanding of the implications of being how you are. The reason you would do this is to ensure that you facilitate the functioning of the rest of the organisation as opposed to getting in the way. Whilst other people can help in this process, as you are the CEO only you can manage it.

In Chapter 7 we will talk about distinct individuals and their styles and approach and we suggest the use of a form of behavioural profiling called MBTI and other instruments. You need to know how you stand against these instruments because this part of your profile will need to be shared with at least those people you interact with directly in the organisation. If you don't do this you will not be helping everyone else to understand how you operate. The more in depth parts of your personality such as your underlying beliefs do not need to be shared but you need to be fully aware of them as they will effect how you act and respond to others.

In short hand terms here are outline examples of the styles of two types of CEO:

Command and Control - the simplest form of this type of profile is a military commander who issues orders and expects them to be followed without question. This is an exclusive

Chapter 4 - The self-aware CEO

style. Others are not encouraged to contribute and the performance of the organisation can be almost totally reliant on what one person says. However you may well find at the bottom of the organisation that these instructions are not followed because they don't work and they don't make sense. A way is found to get round them without telling the CEO.

Pastoral Shepherd - there are CEOs who operate on the basis of believing the staff can perform effectively and grow into the spaces they need to occupy without the issue of direct instructions. The expectation is that people share the business's overall objectives and know how to adapt what they are doing to ensure that they are achieved. They feel that issuing direct instructions will interfere with the learning each individual needs to go through to enhance their contribution. The danger is that nothing happens in the way in which the CEO would wish.

The above constitute two extremes. If you as the CEO don't identify with either please do not be surprised. What you do need to do is to correctly identify what your style and approach is so that you have a good understanding of how it may impact on everyone else. You can then ask for feedback as to whether your impression of what you do is what the rest of the organisation actually sees.

There is no one style of being a CEO. You need to understand what yours is so you can manage it the most effective way. Finding out the impact it has on others will enable you to develop your style.

What we are suggesting takes courage. It takes the CEO out of the comfort zone of being the authority figure in charge of everything. The benefits and rewards of this approach should be that you get more involvement from other people in the success of the business (see Chapter 5) and they will help you achieve what you want to achieve. You don't want them fighting what you are trying to achieve or doing their own thing because they don't believe you have got it right or because they can't be bothered.

Chapter 4 - The self-aware CEO

The CEO and the Management Team

The group of people with whom the CEO has the most interaction tends to be the management team. Every CEO needs to understand their impact on this collection of individuals. It is likely that they will be a group of strong, often independently minded people who for the most part have a high degree of belief in their own abilities. Strong people are more difficult to manage than run of the mill people. The CEO needs to understand what kind of strong people populate the management team in order to know how to get the best out of them.

We talk about genuine teamwork in Chapter 8. This clearly needs to apply to the Management Team. There is at this level a greater likelihood of competition between the team members particularly amongst those ambitious enough to want to succeed the CEO. Somehow the efforts of all these people need to be aligned towards achieving the business's objectives rather than just their personal ones. Competition in itself is not a negative thing provided that it is channelled effectively for the best interests of the business. We would however emphasise that collaboration is more important and far more productive than competition and the CEO should try to manage the team in this direction. Indeed a senior manager who cannot behave collaboratively with his peers and their teams will detract from bottom-line profit. This is not a good indicator for that person's future success as a CEO. Positively managing this collection of people will be significantly aided by understanding their personal styles and approaches.

CEOs need to be very careful about giving greater weight to people who share their own style and approach. Such people will respond to situations in the same way that the CEO does. Hence it is easy for their views to be given greater value than they are worth. Other people who have far less similarity with the CEO's style may not always be fully understood. Understanding their styles and approaches should help in framing questions to elicit what is really concerning them. There is also a tendency for CEOs to value people with a very dissimilar profile as this may complement the way the CEO does things. Care needs to be taken that positive responses to what these people say are not just given as a matter of course without thinking through the consequences.

Chapter 4 - The self-aware CEO

As we will outline in Chapter 8, Genuine Teamwork, the most effective teams have a mixture of styles and approaches. CEOs may find that there tends to be less of a mixture in management teams as certain styles are more prevalent amongst the senior management community. This can often mean that the management team is a lot less cohesive than it needs to be for the benefit of the organisation. The team should be working collectively to find how best to manage the consequences of any lack of cohesion that exists.

Example 2 – Everyone agrees with the CEO?

There is a well know instance where the CEO of General Motors was holding a management meeting. In discussing a certain issue he found that everyone agreed with a particular course of action. His response was to send everyone home to think again. He said that the absence of disagreement may well have meant that the management team had reached the wrong decision.

Effective management teams have constructive disagreements as a necessary tool for ensuring that issues have been properly tested. This should ensure that the solutions agreed will work since the alternatives have been fully examined.

Decision making

Different organisations have different decision making frameworks. Whatever the framework, and whoever makes the decisions, they need to be doing it in a connected and cohesive manner. This means consulting other affected parties, paying attention to the needs of customers and keeping an eye on where the business as a whole is trying to get to.

The CEO needs to provide encouragement for decisions to be taken in this way so that it becomes a standard expectation that this is how it is done.

Sometimes emergency action is required. In these cases a different decision making approach may be necessary. Care should be taken that this does not spill over onto decisions which require connected and cohesive decision making. Putting out a fire should

Chapter 4 - The self-aware CEO

not cause you to have a knee-jerk reaction about how to stop it happening again. This requires careful consideration with others of the various options and the impacts they may have.

There is no manual that tells you how to make judgements. Encouraging people to make judgements in the right way is the most that anyone can do. The right way is to make use of their experience, expertise and skill and ensuring that they are making an informed judgement by ensuring that they have consulted the right people and considered the consequences. All CEOs will have made good and bad judgements through their career and have some understanding of what differentiates between the two. Other people need to be encouraged to learn the same lessons.

Purpose and direction

Most people would agree that a key part of the CEO's role is to establish and sustain the organisation's purpose and direction. It is the specific nature of the purpose and direction that drives the bottom-line of the organisation and its behaviour. If this at any stage becomes unclear, the organisation will suffer as a result. This lack of clarity will quickly pass to everyone else without formal communication being necessary, therefore undermining the linkages and connections that have been carefully built up. The organisation's performance will as a consequence be skewed away from the path it is supposed to be following.

The cohesive approach that we outline in this book defines the state of mind that needs to be used to achieve the required results. You can use this state of mind whatever the required results are, but the way in which you apply it will be different in each case. The CEO's role is to ensure that the various aspects of the organisation operate in a way that delivers the cohesion that is needed. The greater the lack of cohesion is, the worse the bottom-line results.

It is also worth saying that the CEO needs to ensure that the nature of the organisation's bottom-line is clear to everyone. Profit today does not necessarily lead to profit tomorrow.

Chapter 4 - The self-aware CEO

There is a need to be clear on what the bottom-line is in a short, medium and long term sense and that it relates to the organisation.

If the nature of the purpose, direction and bottom-line are clear, then anyone working on a strategy for a particular function can relate it to these items. They can then achieve an effective result by applying the tenets of the cohesive organisation outlined in this book.

The greatest danger is uncertainty. This results in effort being lost, diverted and wasted and hence has a very negative impact on the bottom-line.

Facilitating change

However well your organisation is performing, at some point change will become necessary. This may be new systems, new production techniques, a change in the market place, mergers and acquisitions, or new political directives. In all these circumstances the way things are done in the organisation (organisational culture) will be an important factor in how that change needs to be handled. We explain in Chapter 10 that the culture is not something the CEO directly controls. Culture happens, and the more people there are in the organisation the more it can happen by accident rather than by design. To change this culture requires everyone in the organisation to be involved in that change.

In our experience the most positive results arise when the CEO is a facilitator of change rather than the person who tells everyone what they need to do differently.

By facilitation we mean making sure the overall direction and key parameters are clear and then encouraging all appropriate people to play their part in achieving the change objectives. If you already have a cohesive organisation that has the state of mind that we outline in this book, changes will be carried through effectively and speedily. This should even apply if a cutback is required so long as it is a genuine one that everyone sees the need for. This is provided that anyone who needs to leave the organisation as a consequence is selected according to agreed criteria and is supported in a positive manner.

Chapter 4 - The self-aware CEO

If the organisation is not cohesive in itself then handling change successfully will always be more difficult to achieve. In any event, whilst making major changes, 15% -20% of performance is likely to be lost through people worrying about or discussing their futures, and delays in decision making through uncertainty.

Summary

The self aware CEO is an essential part of a cohesive organisation. This not only means knowing yourself but knowing the people you work with and the impact you have on them. Your effectiveness can only be achieved through what other people do. The way you lead will be an important determining factor in whether others follow.

The following chapters describe elements of the holistic approach that you will need to facilitate. By doing this consistently over a long period of time you will give vital support to others who take the lead in particular areas within your organisation. You need to know the principles behind each of these elements.

Chapter 5 - Everyone owns the bottom-line

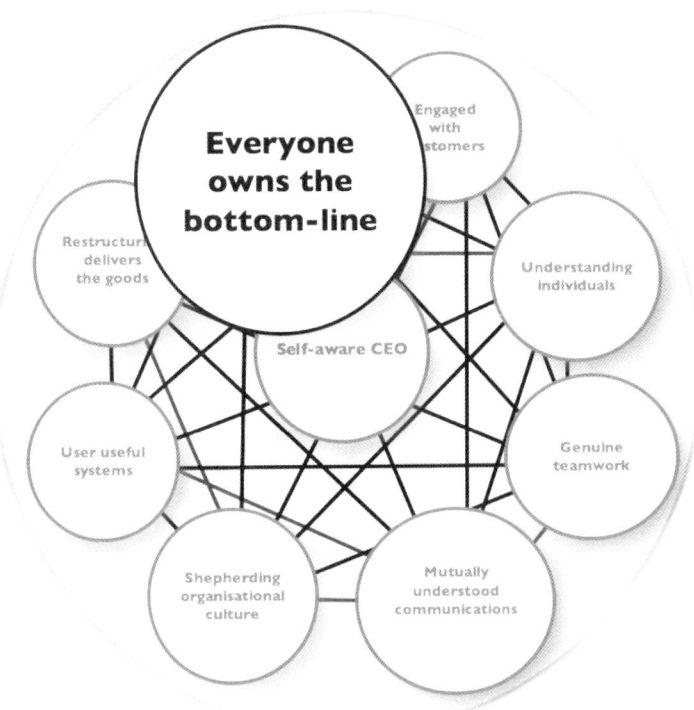

The issue

Common sense suggests that organisations whose parts link together will produce superior outcomes and profits. To achieve this everyone needs to work cooperatively towards the bottom-line. If people are working to their own agendas the consequent lack of cohesion will inevitably impact negatively on the bottom-line outcome.

It is necessary to achieve this culture of collaborative behaviour rather than one of internal competition. However in our experience competition is more prevalent than collaboration. The ability to collaborate with one another is the first and possibly the most important missing link in many organisations.

Chapter 5 - Everyone owns the bottom-line

Defining the bottom-line: - profit/end results

Profit as a measure of bottom-line performance is seen to be very much a feature of Private Sector organisations. For this reason the present Chapter focuses largely on commercial activity. However Public Sector organisations also have bottom-line results to achieve but they are measured in a different way. The issue of managing organisational cohesion to maximise results in the Public Sector is dealt with specifically in Chapter 13.

When discussing profit we prefer a simple notion rather than more complex ones. The easier profit is to understand by everyone in an organisation the greater the possibilities of a cohesive approach to managing it. The definition we advocate is:

> "Profit is what you get when you subtract all forms of expenditure from all forms of income".

The challenge is how to maximise the income from those things that generate it whilst at the same time reducing those that cost you money. Too often we have seen situations where organisations dealing with bottom-line issues only focus on the expenditure side of the equation without any consideration of how to improve income.

Defining the bottom-line: - indirect contributions

Not everyone in an organisation contributes directly to financial profit but they do contribute to bottom-line results.

You can express the function of every overhead operation in such a way that it is connected to the bottom-line and the needs of the organisation in ways other than just how it manages its budget. For example the HR function exists to recruit, retain, develop and reward people with the necessary skills to meet the needs of the organisation (the important words in this statement are "the needs of the organisation" i.e. that enable bottom-line results to be produced).

Whilst writing this section the following example happened to occur:

Chapter 5 - Everyone owns the bottom-line

> Example 3 – Impact of failing to deliver
>
> A phone call was received to say that some furniture could not be delivered because it had not been received in the local warehouse. Apparently a pallet of furniture had been sent to the wrong place. The question is - did the fork lift truck driver who loaded the pallet understand that this mistake could have a negative impact on the bottom line? This could include a loss of future sales because of the organisation's failure to deliver on the commitments it made to the customer.

In this simple but, as it happened, timely example, the bottom-line is affected in two ways. Extra expense is incurred because of the failure in the system first time round and there is an increased financial risk of losing future income because of customer dissatisfaction. In the example above how well did fork lift truck driver understand that what they do has an impact on the bottom line? Were the consequences of their actions explained to them? Were any further checks carried out to make sure the fault didn't lie elsewhere? N.b. This is not about allocating blame. It is about learning from a situation and avoiding a repetition.

This reinforces the point that both qualitative and quantitative data shed light onto factors that hold organisations and their clients together. Information is not numbers, numbers are part of information. People need to see and understand the wider picture otherwise they are not able to tune their contributions to the benefit of the whole business. Understanding and discussing qualitative issues such as client and staff attitudes, complaints, client and business retention and competitive factors adds dimension and depth to statistical reporting.

Who owns your bottom-line?

Everyone should do, of course!

So:

Your bottom-line is where the complexities of your organisation come together. It reflects how well your organisation is working together towards the same goals. It is where ultimately your success is measured by your stakeholders and the public.

We have found in many organisations in which we have worked that there is an absence of focus on end results. Many people seem engrossed in their own concerns relating to

Chapter 5 - Everyone owns the bottom-line

their specific job or department. Their effort goes into following processes and systems without awareness of how these connect with bottom-line results. The real purpose of doing things is often ignored. It seems to us this is an example of "it's not my problem. The bottom-line is something other people look after - not me".

Example 4 – Long term as well as short term bottom-line

The recent crisis in the banking sector has illustrated how careful you need to be when rewarding staff. High level bonuses were earned on the basis of significant short term bottom-line gains. The consequence was a negative effect on the longer term bottom-line. It became apparent that many loans that had been made were not going to be repaid because the customers lacked the capacity to repay them. This was not a short term lending issue but was a longer term one. If the scheme for rewarding these bankers had been properly connected to the longer term bottom-line their focus might well have been different. If so the banks might not have crashed or required rescuing.

In a cohesive organisation everyone owns the bottom-line, understands what it has to be and accepts a shared responsibility for it. In such organisations, people not only understand this responsibility but know how to exercise it.

There are organisations such as the UK retailer, John Lewis, where every employee is a partner in the business and personally benefits from the organisation's success. We would say that there is much greater potential to engage these staff with the bottom-line than those in organisations where such links are not the case.

A clear practical example of such behaviour is that in a situation of global economic difficulty the workforces in many organisations have agreed to pay cuts. They have also agreed to change working practices to keep the organisation afloat and to protect their own jobs in the longer run.

Can everyone in your organisation articulate their sense of ownership of and contribution to your bottom-line? If they can't, this is a missing link. It means something has not been effectively communicated and/or understood.

Chapter 5 - Everyone owns the bottom-line

Accounting & measurement

In working towards bottom-line achievement, cohesive organisations have accountants who look at things in the wider context. They advise other managers on the best way to achieve what they are aiming for, rather than trying to dominate financial matters. This role emphasises cohesion rather than control.

Effective accountants do not control expenditure; they avoid under all circumstances the temptation to be information hoarders. Sharing information, rather than hoarding it, is what creates real collective power in organisations.

The way that money is budgeted and used is the responsibility of the managers to whom budgets have been allocated. The same applies to responsibility for revenue generation. Successful managers are in control of their finances and know what they are doing and where they are going. They also ask for and receive appropriate advice from finance specialists. It is of vital importance that financial systems support managers in this regard. They need to record forward commitments rather than merely accounting for what has already happened. This is important because it shows the true level of expenditure that is committed (i.e. it has been decided to spend) and a clearer picture of what finance is available. If this can be extended to include information for several years ahead it will support effective longer term decision making.

We have come across situations where the Financial Controller has tried to assume responsibility for expenditure in an organisation. Without exception this has been an unmitigated failure because they do not have the direct knowledge or responsibility needed to perform this function. They lack understanding of the consequences of making or not making that expenditure. It is all too easy to find an apparently cheaper solution which involves a reduction in the quality of the items concerned with consequent knock-on failure costs. In a cohesive organisation people from different areas of expertise work together to find the actions that will deliver the optimum benefits to the organisation.

Chapter 5 - Everyone owns the bottom-line

> *Example 5 – Increasing prices may not be the answer*
>
> *A public sector museum in the UK was experiencing losses against its set budget. The accountant involved proposed to increase the admission charges to balance the books. The route taken by management was to reduce the charges so that they were at a level that was affordable to families and hence would increase the number of visits made. The result was an increase in the number of admissions which enabled the books to be balanced.*
>
> *In a similar vein a small private sector museum in Eastern England was struggling to make ends meet. It was decided to remove admission charges and to give free entrance. The net result was a substantial increase in the numbers of people visiting the museum and takings from the sales of gifts and refreshments far exceeded the previous total takings, including the admission charges.*

The above two examples show how thinking about ways of maximising income as well as of reducing costs can produce a different approach to an issue. This potentially generates a result that better meets the organisation's needs rather than simply cutting costs.

Competition or collaboration?

An issue we continuously meet in organisations is that of internal competition. By its very nature internal competition is rarely about competing bids to make the bottom-line bigger. It is more about establishing or increasing individual status, promotion prospects or power and influence than it is to do with company results. Collaboration needs some joint purpose to succeed. This purpose should be working together to optimise that bottom-line.

In the myths and beliefs identified in Chapter 2 the persistent thread is that the workplace is an essentially divided place. In itself division of labour is not a bad thing. However it can have unforeseen consequences. At its worst a tribal culture can result leading to much energy being dissipated in competitive, if not destructive, activities. This means that you disappoint customers, create internal inefficiencies and lose money.

Some organisations delude themselves into believing that internal competition somehow delivers the best results. What they fail to recognise is the enormous failure costs

Chapter 5 - Everyone owns the bottom-line

associated with internal strife and how this lack of cohesion and focus in their business actually undermines bottom-line results.

For clarity, 'Failure cost' is the cost of what has been done wrong and the cost of putting it right. It may be as simple as the cost of having to redo a job because of ineffective communication. It may be as serious as the massive costs of failing to control financial risk. In all cases failure cost hits bottom-line performance negatively.

Example 6 – Failure costs can be higher than you think

Work carried out by one of us in the insurance sector showed that approximately 40% of management expenses in a particular company were attributable to failure cost! If this seems like a large number, some research we undertook at the time indicated that it was not unusual in the banking sector for this figure to be even higher.

Failure cost is often a consequence of a culture of divide and rule, of personality clashes, of professional jealousies or even of deliberate succession planning tactics!

Example 7 – Internal competition can lead to inter-departmental warfare

An organisation we worked with managed its succession planning process by getting three senior executives to function in a competitive way with each other to see which one would come out on top. The immediate consequence of this was that the teams reporting to the executives ended up in fierce and destructive internal competition with one another. This resulted amongst other things in dangerous investment decisions being made and focus being taken off the market place. The longer term consequence was that the organisation failed financially and ended up being acquired by one of its external competitors.

Cohesive budgeting,

The budgetary process which is at the heart of goal setting for the bottom-line is very much about achieving cohesion and shared goals. It provides a financial structure that is an integral part of the framework by which individuals and teams across an organisation make common cause to deliver shared goals.

Chapter 5 - Everyone owns the bottom-line

A collaborative approach to budgeting is not a competitive scramble for resources. It is a process facilitated by accountants in which managers should think strategically and actively cooperate with each other.

Example 8 – Determining budgets cohesively

A company refined its budgetary process to focus on shared business outcomes to be achieved across the whole team. The aim was also to get it right first time. Their start point was the amount of capital invested in the business and the return required on it by the shareholders. This set the bottom-line profit goal to be achieved. Significant effort went into working out the likely income from all sources. This then identified how much money could be spent given the return that was needed on capital employed. The budgetary exercise then focused on the management team deciding collaboratively how to divide this between areas to best achieve the income goals. Each manager went away knowing what their budget was and why. They had to decide within their teams how this could best be used. No games. No failure costs to deal with by not getting it right first time. A cohesive approach.

Interestingly the business reinforced its financial processes by being very open and informative in its internal communications. By sharing how it was performing against goals, ownership was reinforced and its people felt a key part of outcomes. The bottom-line profit increased significantly.

This particular process encapsulates for us the fundamental point that bottom-line profit is achieved through management collaboration. It does not just happen. It requires you and your team to work together not to fight each other.

In our experience the CEO needs to reinforce the importance of cooperation and to stop any tendency by managers to look after their own interests rather than the interests of the whole organisation. This makes best use of people's time and efforts and has the most positive impact on the bottom-line.

Understanding the bottom-line

Both qualitative and quantitative data shed light onto factors that hold organisations and their clients together. Relying on only one or the other form of data limits the picture available to managers. So you must include qualitative information when measuring the bottom-line. Remember that information is not numbers, numbers are part of information.

Chapter 5 - Everyone owns the bottom-line

Cohesiveness and effectiveness in organisations are not just measured by classic numeric information but by more subtle and complex data on issues such as client and staff attitudes, complaints, client and business retention and competitive factors. This can be harder to gather than numbers. If its value is not exploited and understood across the organisation, then it becomes all too convenient to fall back on measures that are easier to gather even though they do not provide a complete picture.

People need to see and understand the wider picture otherwise they are not able to tune their contributions to the benefit of the whole business. Understanding and discussing the qualitative issues adds dimension and depth to statistical reporting.

For example an organisation could be consistently making profits but is about to lose its best staff through retirement. It also needs to replace its IT systems and manufacturing processes because they are out of date. The quantitative position is that the organisation is healthy whereas the actual position is that the organisation is in imminent danger of failing substantially.

Example 9 – Historical successes and failures

IBM was a very successful provider of mainframe computers that took a major hit when personal computers appeared. Kodak was a world leader in camera films that was badly affected by the advent of digital photography. Olympia Business Machines was a very successful producer of typewriters until computers came on the scene. Whilst all these companies have survived they experienced significant hits to their bottom-lines. In all these cases the accounting measures indicated positive results but the overall picture was quite different.

Summary

For an organisation to gain the maximum benefit from its potential, everyone in it needs to share in ownership of the bottom-line. This bottom-line is not just the amount of profit the organisation makes but those other aspects that contribute to sustaining its health and success into the future.

Chapter 5 - Everyone owns the bottom-line

In order to achieve this the organisation needs to be engaged with its customers. If they don't buy the organisation's products and services it will cease to exist. We turn to this in our next chapter.

In addition for each individual to share in ownership of the bottom-line, they need to feel that their contribution is properly understood and valued by the organisation. We turn to this in Chapter 7.

Chapter 6 - Engaged with customers

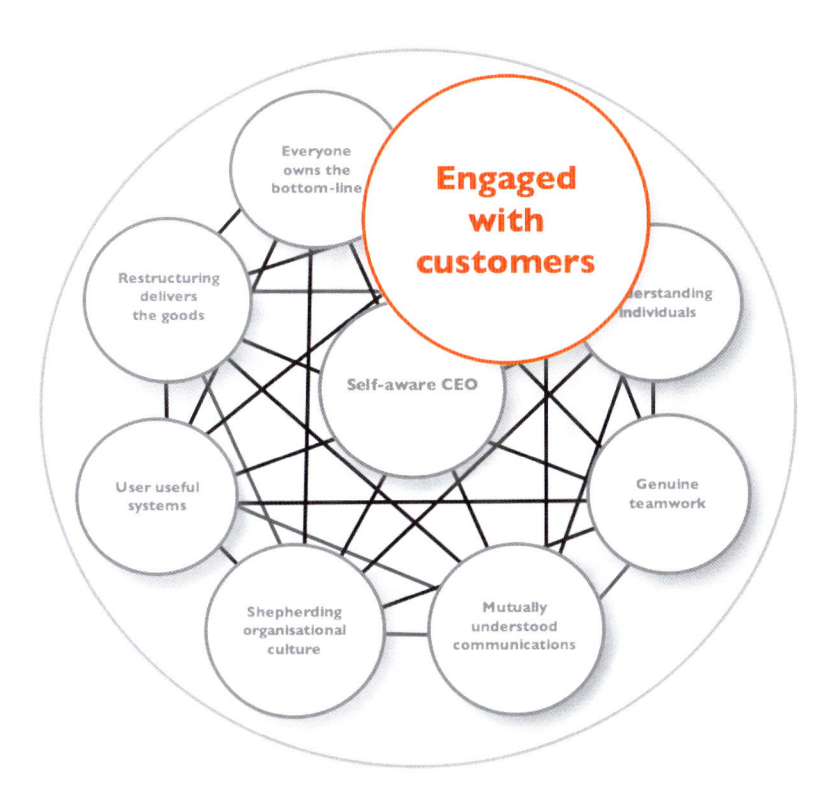

The Issue

Engaging with your customer means making every effort to ask your customer what they want. You then need to ensure in conjunction with them that what you provide is what they want. Making sure that everyone in the organisation is aligned in a cohesive manner will deliver this result, the customer will recognise this and feel they received the product or service they wanted. Without this you do not have a sustainable bottom-line.

There are countless examples of organisations that say that they do this whilst actually doing the opposite. They make assumptions about what the customer wants; they haven't asked the customer what they actually want. They are providing what it suits their organisation to provide. Such organisations will often say that they are giving customer

Chapter 6 - Engaged with customers

service but they are NOT engaging with customers, they are treating them as almost incidental.

Consistent customer propositions

Your organisation needs to be able to back up, by its actions, the statements being made to customers otherwise it will create confusion and dissent both among customers and within the organisation itself. People recognise when an organisation doesn't mean what it says. This is a clear example of a missing link.

Our central contentions are:

- Whilst you decide what customer proposition you are going to offer, the customer decides whether they want it.

- If you have understood the market properly your proposition will be taken up by sufficient customers to make it worthwhile.

- Your organisation must operate in a way that is wholly connected to the proposition.

The clearest example that comes to mind is:

Example 10 – A clear customer proposition

Ronseal, a UK subsidiary of the US Sherwin-Williams Company, market their exterior wood-stains, wood-dyes, and furniture care products under the strap line:

"It does exactly what it says on the tin"

Customers should expect no less than "it does exactly what it says on the tin" from any organisation.

This does not mean that the product or service has to be expensive, or the best on the market. It means it has to be consistently what it says it is. For example:

Chapter 6 - Engaged with customers

> *Example 11 – A consistent customer value proposition*
>
> Ryanair brands itself as "Ryanair, Fly Cheaper". It describes itself on its website as the 'Cheap Flights-Lowest European Fares, Low Cost Airline'.
>
> If you want extras you pay for them. The success of this organisation is an ample demonstration that it is tuned into a sector of the market place which is happy to buy the low cost proposition. People do so in sufficient numbers for the organisation to generate profits. They do not expect Ryanair to be a 'full service' airline.

Ensure your marketing people develop campaigns or use slogans that can be followed through by the rest of the organisation. Any mismatch quickly becomes obvious to clients, your people and ultimately the general public. This is well summarised by:

> *Example 12 – Not doing what you say that you are doing*
>
> The Marketing Department of a major Australian insurance group spent several million dollars to develop a customer campaign. This was based on the advertising slogan "For the most important person in the world - you!" The campaign contrasted the treatment of people as 'statistics' by other institutions with the way they would be treated as 'individuals' by the insurance company concerned. Unfortunately, despite the slogan and the expensive advertising, the organisation's own customer systems were only capable of identifying its customers by their policy number - not their name. It was not long before the public identified that the company was incapable of delivering its marketing hype. The marketing spend was therefore wasted money.

Your organisation's behaviour needs to be consistent with what you say you are giving to your customers (i.e. your customer value proposition). The creativity of your marketing needs to be linked to the reliability of your product and service teams, and the people orientation of your call centres. It is no good for one of these to be good on its own. All must be good at the same time.

We have observed many companies that do not manage the customer relationship effectively across their business operations. This often results in inconsistent service and

Chapter 6 - Engaged with customers

frustrates and loses customers the organisation has spent large amounts of money on to attract to their business. Hence resources are wasted, time is lost, and customers are dissatisfied and move elsewhere. The bottom-line suffers as a result.

The most important people

Who are the most important people in your organisation as far as your customers are concerned? These are the ones on the front line.

Who do we mean by this? We mean those staff who have direct contact with your customers, they are the start of your income stream. The receptionist, the call-centre operators, the sales people, and those dealing with customer queries and complaints are the most important. The rest of the organisation, including the chief executive, should be aligned behind them to support their efforts.

Why do we think these are the most important people. The right words from these staff are most likely to secure a sale which in turn is likely to lead to repeat sales in the future. A wrong word by them can not only lose you a sale but can cause you to lose many more sales as the customer shares their bad experiences with family, friends and colleagues.

Why is it then that call-centre staff are often given a script with which they have to follow when talking to the customer? This takes no account of individual customer needs and doesn't encourage your staff to listen to the customer. It also implies that the staff you employ are not to be trusted and are unable to respond flexibly to what the customer wants. To quote a jargon phrase "one size does not fit all". Customers are individuals the same as your members of staff are. If they don't receive good personal service you may regret it for a long time. Your system is of no importance to the customer, it delivers no more benefits than the customers expect when they phone up.

So are you connected with what happens on the front line? If not go and experience it for yourself. Do not rely on one of your managers giving you the answer he or she thinks you want to hear.

Chapter 6 - Engaged with customers

If you have visited the front line and found a problem, please resist the temptation to go for instant blanket solutions. You will need to engage with your staff and understand your organisation's culture to enable an effective solution to be produced. We will turn to these issues in later Chapters.

Many UK organisations have in recent years transferred customer call-centres overseas, often for reasons of cost. In the UK there has been a great deal of negative reaction to these moves because customers are often unable to get the positive reactions they need from staff in these call-centres. It is clear that in many instances the staff have not been trained properly. Little account has been taken of the difference in cultures between the overseas location and the UK. Assumptions have been made about both the skills of the staff and their ability to understand UK customers. It is not that this cannot work effectively or that the staff in the overseas location are unable to do it effectively. It is that often insufficient time and effort has been invested in this process and no recognition has been made of the need to link two different cultures. It is managing for organisational convenience rather than seeing the situation through the customers' eyes.

Example 13 – A successful foreign call-centre

ANZ, an Australian bank, has a call-centre in India. They have made significant efforts to ensure that the staff in this centre can answer any individual customer query. If they are not able to do this directly they find the answer and call back. This creates a flexible and productive relationship with customers.

Retention of customers

Organisations need to consider whether there is more value to them in the retention of existing customers or the acquisition of new ones. If you are offering a consistent customer proposition that they like shouldn't you be endeavouring to retain them? You have invested time and effort in this process in the expectation of generating sustainable value to the bottom-line.

Chapter 6 - Engaged with customers

It is interesting to note that a fairly common practice in the financial services and insurance markets is a concentration on rewarding new customers better than established ones. New customers are offered discounted rates, lower premiums and special interest deals on transferring debt and credit.

If everyone in the marketplace follows this practice what is to stop your existing customers transferring their allegiance to other organisations to gain 'new customer benefits'. They can then transfer again and again accruing further benefits for ever and a day. Doesn't this put everyone's' costs up and destroy customer loyalty. Is it a race to the bottom?

Would it actually be better to reward those customers who have cost you money to acquire and with whom you have established a relationship?

In our view these organisations have a disconnected customer proposition. This is contrary to the concept of a cohesive organisation. It has a negative effect on the bottom-line.

Summary

To engage with your customers you need:

- A differentiated product or service which can be presented as a consistent customer value proposition.

- You need to have consulted with and gained feedback from your customers.

- All parts of your business operation need to be aligned to supporting your customer proposition.

- Each person's actions need to be consistent with this.

In the next Chapter we look at how you can understand the individuals in your organisation to help them support these business efforts.

Chapter 7 - Understanding individuals

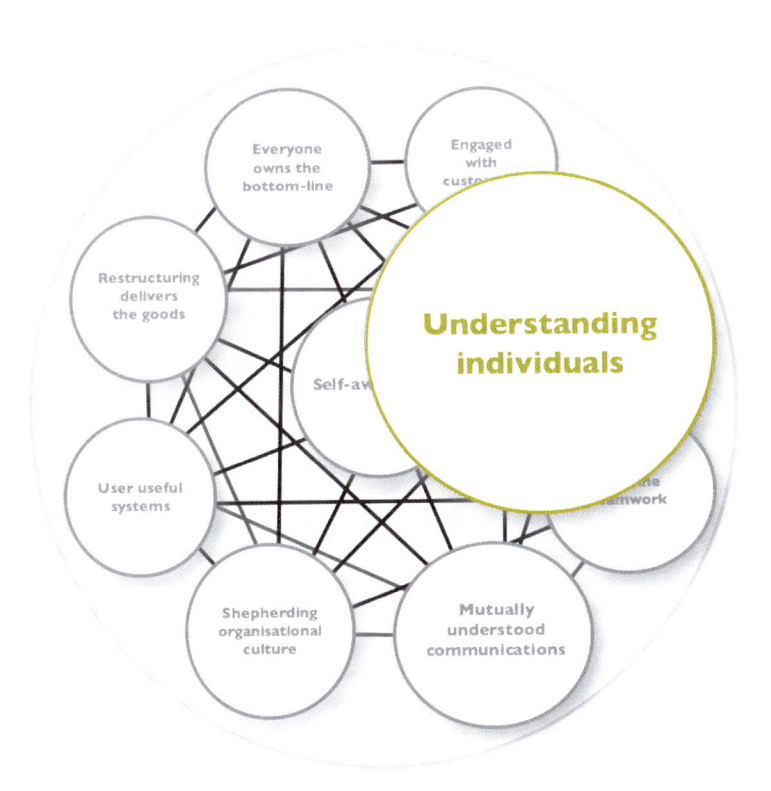

The issue

In cohesive organisations individuals' distinct skills and approaches are understood, recognised and valued. People are not seen merely as cogs in a machine but for what their contribution adds to the effectiveness of the organisation. Differences are appreciated not frowned on. Cohesive organisations understand where individuals are coming from and what their distinct contribution is.

Individual distinct approaches

In a cohesive organisation everyone endeavours to understand everyone else's individual approach. In doing so the likelihood of the most beneficial bottom-line results occurring is optimised.

Chapter 7 - Understanding individuals

So how do you identify these distinct approaches?

When it comes to those who are most familiar to us i.e. our family and friends we know that they are all different. We know there are ways of saying things to each of them that will generate a positive, a negative or a disinterested response. What one person enjoys another will hate. Why is it that when considering people in organisations all of this learning is so often forgotten or sidelined? It is as if recognising individuals' distinct behaviour has become too difficult.

We all have a tendency to categorise people in some way shape or form. For instance people are short, tall, fat, thin, male and female, of one ethnic group or another. Within organisations we categorise people as being helpful, cooperative, awkward, difficult, bossy, detail minded, good with people, hard to get on with, decisive, indecisive, all over the place etc..etc...In so doing we all have a different framework of descriptions that we use according to our own understanding of ourselves and what we would do in a set of given circumstances. If someone else behaves differently we may think that it is not 'right' or that it is better or worse than what we would do rather than being just different.

If we are to treat people as the organisation's greatest asset we need to understand the differences between individuals. Only then can we determine what value those differences add. To do this we need to have a common language, a kind of standard set of definitions that get round the problem of the myriads of individual criteria that we have all created for ourselves. This will then enable a shared understanding of the different things that each individual brings.

A basis for understanding that we have found works best is the Myers Briggs Type Indicator (MBTI®). This describes an individual's cognitive style and approach i.e. the way they think about things and the approach they use when taking action. A person's 'type' is an inherent part of their make-up. They use it as part of their 'tool kit' to address whatever issues and problems they face. The following is a simplified short description of what MBTI® 'types' consist of:

Chapter 7 - Understanding individuals

There are four pairs of preferences. Each individual is on one side or the other of each of these pairs. The pairs are:

Extrovert – their energy comes from inter-action with people or things (E)
Introvert – their energy is internal (I)

Sensing – focus on facts and concrete issues located in the present and follow through steps in dealing with them (S)
Intuition – focus on possibilities about where things are headed in the future and follow through mental jumps in dealing with them (N)

Thinking – take decisions using logic and analysis arriving at the 'correct' answer (T)
Feeling – take decisions using a personal value set, with an eye to harmony, arriving at the 'right' answer (F)

Judging – prefer a life style of order, planning and closure (J)
Perceiving – prefer a life style of flexibility, spontaneity and openness (P)

Each person's type consists of four letters, one each from the pairs identified above. For information about the various type combinations please refer to the following recommended titles:

> An Introduction to Type® - European English Edition by Isabel Briggs Myers pub. Consulting Psychologists Press Inc. 1055 Joaquin Road, 2nd Floor, Mountain View, CA 94043 USA 2000

> An Introduction to Type® and Teams by Elizabeth Hirsh, Katherine W Hirsh, and Sandra Krebs Hirsh pub. Consulting Psychologists Press Inc. 1055 Joaquin Road, 2nd Floor, Mountain View, CA 94043 USA 2003

Using the MBTI® enables people to understand where they are in relation to a common framework. They learn in what way they may be different to other people they work with. Used in an individual and team context it allows these differences to be explored without

Chapter 7 - Understanding individuals

prejudice and in an impersonal way. So what should emerge is an understanding of why you find other people valuable or irritating so that you can find the true worth of what they are talking about. There is no inherent right or wrong type but there may be certain types who are better in certain situations than other types. But no type is better in every situation.

The MBTI® has been successfully translated into a wide variety of languages and adjusted to allow for cultural differences. Hence it works in all cultures and all countries. It can therefore provide a unifying influence where people are valued for who they are, not where they have come from.

Implication of personal differences

Whatever your 'profile'(MBTI® type) might be, you will approach things in that way; it is your natural way of doing things. Each person's profile is an integral part of the way they do their work. It is their approach. It can be the reason why they are given particular pieces of work or not, and why they don't see eye to eye with a colleague who has a distinctly different profile. By understanding these differences people learn more about the value that they add to an organisation and the different values that others add. They can also develop their approach better knowing where they are starting from.

In terms of missing links within an organisation, any individual's lack of understanding of where other individuals are coming from and why they behave in different ways causes gaps in understanding, delays and arguments. All of these can be extremely counter-productive to optimising bottom-line performance. These kinds of differences often lie behind why for example the Marketing Department doesn't understand the Production Department and why neither of them gets on with the Finance and HR Departments. Each profession tends to attract a majority of people of particular types (but not exclusively so).

Does this mean that you must have a particular profile to be a successful manager? The answer is no. Any of the types can occupy management positions. However some people's styles will be less easily understood, particularly if they are different from the well understood traditional 'command and control' types. Knowing where you are different enables you to best manage how that comes across to others.

Chapter 7 - Understanding individuals

The MBTI® is a major building block. As you will see in further chapters it can be used not only to understand individuals but to understand team behaviours, organisational culture and the cultures of each country.

Assessing behavioural approaches when appointing people

Appointment decisions are some of the most difficult decisions to make. Picking people is not something that you do often. If you get it wrong it is difficult (but not impossible) to undo. An inappropriate appointment can end up costing you a lot of money. Most people believe that they are good at picking other people. Our experience, from a wide variety of organisations, suggests that this not as strongly the case as people might believe.

When selecting people or considering internal promotions, you are making a forecast. As with the weather you won't always get that forecast right. You need to remember that however successful the candidate has previously been at their current and past jobs they have not done the job you are about to give them. You cannot be certain that they are going to be successful. As with weather forecasting the more data you have available to make the forecast, the better the result is likely to be.

There are two parts to the process:

- The first is appointing someone who has the necessary skills and attributes to carry out the duties and responsibilities required.
- The second is someone who will be a suitable 'fit' into the organisation and will contribute positively to increasing cohesive effort.

Assessing a person's skills and attributes is no easy task. Using a single 45 minute interview to appoint someone to a job carries only a 40% success rate. One of the key tricks to improving this is to use a multiplicity of techniques and to use more than one interview. Selection is like a jigsaw puzzle - having half the pieces does not give you the full picture - you need them all to slot into place to do this.

Chapter 7 - Understanding individuals

The key part of people's skills and attributes is their personal style and approach. Especially for senior management appointments you need to find out what this is and whether the candidate understands how to use it effectively. However good anyone is there are things that they are no good at. In the vast majority of cases these will also stem from their style and approach.

We would advocate using three personality measures to assess this. The MBTI® for cognitive style, FIRO-B to assess interpersonal behavioural style (we will talk more about this in the next Chapter) and a more in depth trait based personality inventory. This would enable candidates to be asked questions at interview to test their own understanding of their impact.

There are traps to avoid in the selection process many of which are associated with the person's style and approach. Amongst the most common of these are:

- Cloning - appointing someone who has the same characteristics as you do (e.g. the same MBTI® style) and answer questions in the way you would like them to be answered,

- Appointing someone who is good at the job they are doing and assuming that they can automatically move to the next level. Having the right people in the right places should mean that everyone is currently doing a good job where they are but this doesn't prove that they will be suitable for a more senior role.

- Not appointing people who stand up to you. The difference and the debate may be what you need in the position.

The cost and time commitment of comprehensive selection processes pales into insignificance in comparison to the amount of money you will spend in salary, benefits and on costs, not to mention the effect of the person's impact on your bottom-line. There are often millions of pounds/dollars/euro involved. If you were going to spend such money on a capital project you would dedicate significant time to ensuring you were making the correct decision. If needs be, make use of external expert assistance to complement your judgement.

Chapter 7 - Understanding individuals

'Fit'

Having determined which candidates can do the job, the second part of the process is one of 'which candidate fits the organisation best'?

This can be both a fit within a particular team or a fit within the way the organisation does things. You may decide that someone who doesn't fit is needed in order to move the organisation in a different direction. Care needs to be taken how much the person is different lest you create a situation where they leave everyone else behind and the appointment therefore becomes ineffective. To use a medical analogy it is like the human body rejecting a transplanted organ.

In making your choice, taking the wrong decision costs you money, lots of it, and probably lots of your time too. It will impact negatively on the cohesion you are striving to achieve and could set your organisation back considerably. Your subsequent decisions may also take time to produce positive results as people's trust in your judgement will have been damaged.

Supporting individual development

It should go without saying that organisations ought to support appropriate development activities for their individual employees. This should be relevant to an understanding of and development of their individual characteristics and impact. Developing people appropriately will have a positive impact on bottom line results.

The view is often taken that having reached senior management level, individuals no longer need personal development. If these are some of the most important people in the organisation then they should receive, for example, access to executive coaching to take their performance to higher levels. Such action may also be needed to provide for future managerial succession. This is investment for the future to ensure your organisation continues to have the skills to survive and succeed.

Chapter 7 - Understanding individuals

Motivating individuals

Many statements have been made about how to motivate people and what would increase people's level of motivation. Whenever this is discussed it feels rather like 'why don't people do what I tell them to do'. This causes us to wonder whether many organisations understand motivation and certainly to conclude that many in fact do not know what to do about it.

You cannot motivate people, they motivate themselves. What you can do is to inspire, enthuse, energise and encourage them but in the end they will do things if they want to do them. You need to be conscious of what your impact is on their motivation.

There is only one recognised model of motivation. This is Maslow's 'hierarchy of needs. 'If you have not come across it before it consists of the following:

There are 5 levels

Level 1	physiological needs (e.g. hunger and thirst)
Level 2	safety needs (e.g. shelter and money)
Level 3	love or belongingness (e.g. being valued and experiencing intimacy)
Level 4	esteem (e.g. respect from peers)
Level 5	self-actualisation (e.g. realising your full potential)

Each of the higher levels requires the levels below it to be met.

How these levels of motivation will actually be met will differ for each individual. In common parlance what you might need are 'different strokes for different folks'. We have already referred to the use of FIRO-B and will return to it in the next Chapter. Amongst other things, this will tell you whether an individual needs positive feedback or not and if so how often and from whom.

There may be occasions when individuals feel motivated to act collectively to generate a result which is both beneficial to the organisation and is in their long term interest. For

Chapter 7 - Understanding individuals

example they may be willing to volunteer in hard times, to take a reduction in pay or in working hours. The follow-on issue is how management will enable them to maintain this level of motivation when times improve. Whilst it is true that you can't directly motivate someone you may demotivate them and could destroy them if you make a major surprise move that cuts across their understanding of where they sit within the organisation.

A basic confusion about motivation concerns the issue of remuneration. Money is not a motivator, people have to motivate themselves. This does not stem from how much money they get. It stems from other things which are to do with recognition of the individual and the things they are able to achieve. It may be more about the comparisons they make with others and whether they feel valued as a result.

On the other hand genuine performance bonuses will have a different motivational effect provided that:

- The money is not guaranteed and has to be earned through genuinely superior performance, and
- There is a direct connection between actions taken and rewards given.

However even in this case, where an individual already has sufficient wealth, the mere existence of such performance reward mechanisms may have no effect at all. Also how targets are set will be important as to whether such bonuses have the requisite motivational impact. Too hard a target will mean a lack of incentive to do anything, too easy a target will lead to switch off once the target is reached. You may need to take care about which staff receive bonuses lest it has a negative impact on others who don't.

In a cohesive organisation all individuals need to be recognised for their distinct contribution so that the organisation actually gains the associated benefits. At the end of the day, whatever your organisational practice is, it needs to reinforce everyone's ownership of the bottom-line as described in Chapter 5.

Chapter 7 - Understanding individuals

Taking responsibility for collective treatment of individuals

In certain organisations it seems to be the practice that management take decisions without engaging with, or consulting with, all the individuals. Trade unions are seen as being macho individuals who need to be battled with, as opposed to being representatives of their members. Confrontational situations are often reached too quickly and with the absence of forethought. This is often because actions are taken which seen as clearly inconsistent by others. For example, awarding senior managers high levels of pay increase whilst applying minimal increases, or even decreases, to everyone is not likely to generate a positive response.

In a cohesive organisation management take responsibility for industrial relations, engage with unions where appropriate and see the workforce as a collection of distinct individuals. They are likely to approach difficult situations, such as the need to downsize or cut costs, as problems to be solved jointly with workers' representatives rather than by management decree. They will endeavour to act consistently in their treatment of people at all levels, and consistent with what needs to be achieved for the benefit of the organisation as a whole. This minimises the negative energy produced and optimises the likelihood of the individuals in the workforce responding positively to the suggestions that emerge from these problem solving discussions. In these situations management seek to understand and anticipate individual's difficulties and try to find as many helpful answers to them as possible. Such a climate usually leads to workers and their representatives making suggestions to help the situation as opposed to blocking progress.

By approaching collective issues in this way you are more likely to sustain positive motivation in each and every individual and hence retain their support and focus on the bottom-line as referred to in Chapter 5. Because you have a difficult financial agenda to manage doesn't mean that success will be achieved through a command and control approach. You might get there in the short term but this will have been achieved at a detrimental cost to performance in the longer run, a pyrrhic victory, one obtained at more cost than its benefit.

Chapter 7 - Understanding individuals

Individuals you might do without

There will be occasions when you have appointed a particular person, usually in a senior position, to achieve a particular objective. An example might be that you have employed a 'hatchet person' in order to secure a certain level of expense reduction. When this has been achieved, you need that person to move on as they are unlikely to be able to manage the more stable situation that has now resulted. There will be other examples which are slightly less clear. But it is often the case that organisations at different stages of development need individuals with different styles and approaches.

Apart from this there may be examples of individuals you have inherited whom you may want to do without. We have seen many senior people who are pursuing their own interests and agendas to the potential detriment of the success of the organisation. Such people get in the way of developmental processes, organisational change, cooperative endeavours and, ultimately, the achievement of bottom-line results because 'they are not singing from the same hymn sheet'. These people need to be removed.

Example 14 -Not singing from the same hymn sheet

CEO of General Electric Jack Welch described people whose results were good but who were unable to adhere to the values of the organisation as being 'corrosive' and needing to be got rid of.

The above example is not to say that disagreement and dissension does not have its place, indeed we argue in the next chapter that it does. However, if you have corrosive people in your organisation they need to be actively managed out of it. Whilst this is never easy you will get more positive recognition and support from the rest of the workforce if you take this action than on any other single issue.

In most organisations, especially the bigger ones, there are also people who occupy places where they make no contribution to the bottom-line. These we might refer to as place-men and place-women. Their sole function is to pass orders down the line, comments back up the line and be nominal representatives at meetings. Whilst these

Chapter 7 - Understanding individuals

people are not corrosive they do not add anything to the operations of your business, become blocks and undermine the motivation of those reporting to them.

Example 15 – Removing organisational post-boxes

When reviewing a particular part of the finance department in a public sector organisation, a particular individual was interviewed. He was asked what his function was. His reply was to say that he was 'the manager'. 'Yes' we said, but what does that involve you doing?' The only task we could positively elicit from this individual was that he opened the post and gave it to the relevant section head. Our resultant conclusion was that his post should be removed from the organisation as being unnecessary.

So how do you go about getting rid of people you might be better without? There are two main ways of doing this. These are:

- Sack people and take the consequences.
- Put effort into managing people out using approved processes.

You would use the former in situations where an individual is causing problems that are so severe to the organisation. This would be such that the cost of continuing to employ them whilst following standard processes far outweighs any compensation that might otherwise be paid.

In the vast majority of cases you would use approved processes, but these require time and energy to be expended. The outcome may be that the individuals change their behaviour in such a way that the organisation is able to retain them. If this happens this is clearly a positive result. To this end the objective of disciplinary processes in a cohesive organisation is to ensure that everyone's behaviour is brought into line with what's required. Early intervention is more likely to achieve this. You would then only endeavour to get rid of people who do not positively respond and do not contribute to organisational success.

Chapter 7 - Understanding individuals

Failure to act in respect of individuals who you can truly do without has major negative bottom-line impact. It may mean that other people fail to achieve their objectives because they do not see you succeeding in yours. It calls into question, in their minds, your own competence as a manager.

Summary

For you to connect with your people and for them to connect with one another the following need to apply:

- Each person should be valued for their distinct contribution - their behavioural style should be understood.
- When appointing and promoting people their individual styles and approaches should be understood before they are placed in a new job. The 'fit' of each candidate should similarly be assessed before they are placed.
- Individuals should be developed, including all those at the top of the organisation.
- Each individual is motivated differently and not always in relation to money. Contributions need to be linked to improvements in the bottom-line.
- Management should take overall responsibility for establishing and maintaining positive relationships with the collection of individuals employed by the organisation.
- Harmonious relationships are achieved by **We** not **I** - 'us' not 'us and them'.
- If there are individuals you need to do without, make sure you do without them.

Your staff are truly your greatest asset. Without them you will not achieve any results. Getting the best from them will contribute greatly to realising your organisation's potential.

In the next Chapter we turn to getting cohesion between individuals when they operate in teams.

Chapter 8 - Genuine teamwork

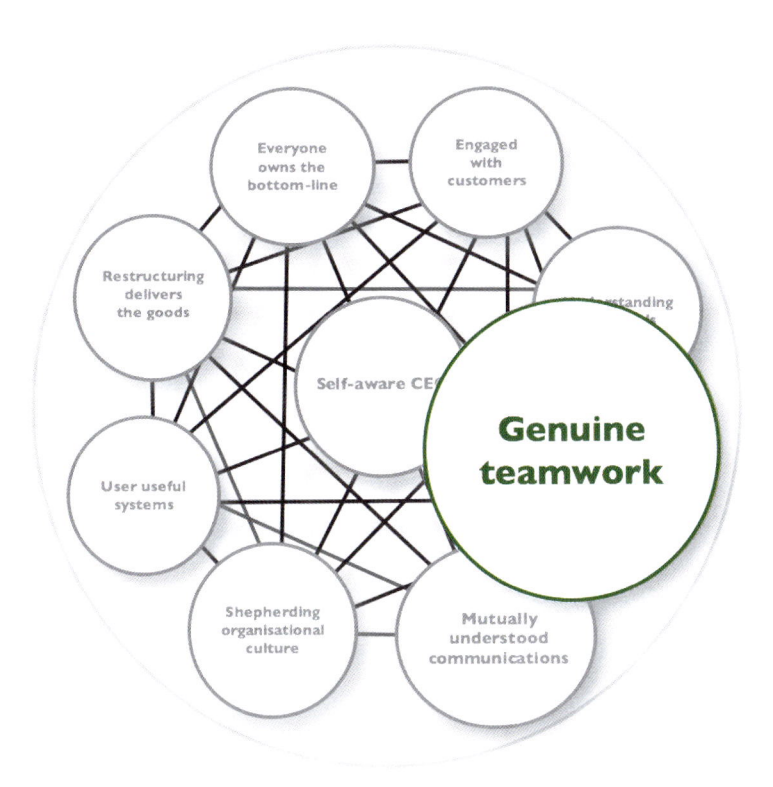

[Diagram: interconnected circles showing "Genuine teamwork" at centre, surrounded by "Everyone owns the bottom-line", "Engaged with customers", "Restructuring delivers the goods", "...standing", "Self-aware CE[O]", "User useful systems", "Shepherding organisational culture", "Mutually understood communications"]

The issue

To gain the most from teams requires an understanding of what drives team behaviour as well as what drives individual behaviour. People in a group will behave differently to their behaviour as individuals. Also the interactions that take place between teams need to be ones of collaboration not competition or the allocation of blame. Optimising these interactions within and between teams leads to joined up working, reduced waste of time and positive impact on the bottom-line.

A basis for understanding teams

Teams are collections of distinct individuals. Organisations therefore need to better understand the collective effect of bringing individuals together into a team. There is often an innate assumption that by labelling a group of people as a 'team' they understand how

Chapter 8 - Genuine teamwork

to behave as one and that they will perform according to expectations. Reality suggests that this is often not the case and that teams do not always work in a cohesive way.

The way in which the team behaves is a result of the particular collection of individuals within it. Altering any member within it will cause the behaviour of the team to change. A simple example of this effect is the way the performance of a football team changes when particular players are or are not playing. They may find it easier or more difficult to pass the ball, keep the ball, defend or score goals. This is because each individual player adds something unique that is not precisely the same as the person they replaced; no two people are alike. It is true that someone will be filling in for their role but will do it differently because they are a different person.

To understand how a team works you need to assess the styles and approaches of each team member. We do this by looking at cognitive style (as measured by MBTI®) and interpersonal behavioural style (as measured by Firo-B). For MBTI® see previous Chapter. For FIRO-B (Fundamental Interpersonal Relationship Orientation - Behaviour) this describes the following:

Inclusion – the extent to which an individual expresses that they wish to be included by others, and the extent to which they want to be included by others

Control – the extent to which an individual expresses a need to be in control (and hence achieve), and the extent to which they want to be controlled by others

Affection – the extent to which people express warmth to others, and the extent to which they want to receive warmth from others.

For further in depth information please refer to:

Clinical Interpretation of the FIRO B by Leo R. Ryan PhD pub. Consulting Psychologists Press Inc. 1055 Joaquin Road, 2nd Floor, Mountain View, CA 94043 USA 1989

The combinations of these MBTI® and FIRO-B will describe the vast majority of the behaviours of individuals within the team.

Chapter 8 - Genuine teamwork

The most effective teams have a wide variety of individual styles and approaches within them. This means that whatever challenges the team faces there is someone who has an approach that fits that problem and can provide the team with the necessary input to solve it. However, in practice, most teams have a preponderance of certain styles and approaches which tend to skew the team's behaviour in that direction. Those within the team who are different to this preponderance may find they have less influence and will be listened to less often because they have a different way of doing things. This is not a cohesive team.

Cohesive teams are ones where each team member understands their style and approach and how it is different from or similar to the other team members. In addition the team will have a collective view of the strengths and gaps inherent within the team as a result of their particular collection of styles and approaches. This then enables the team to take corrective action when necessary by focusing on those gaps and, if needs be, by adding other people in to fill them.

However cohesive a team is, it can quite easily fall into the trap of blaming other teams for problems which occur, often because those teams operate differently. In a cohesive organisation each of these teams should have discussions with the other teams with which they inter-relate to identify the strengths and gaps in the relationship between them. This again then enables both teams concerned to take appropriate action to fill the gaps or to amend how they do things if it will assist the other team by so doing. Clearly this needs to be a genuine two way process in order for that relationship to thrive and prosper.

Much emphasis is placed on the word 'teamwork'. Genuine teamwork requires an understanding of the collective strengths and gaps present within each team and in their relationships with every other team. Different collections of individuals result in different team performances.

The performance of your team, whether it is a senior management team, an operational team or a project team, will equate to the summary of the individual profiles of the team members as measured using MBTI® and FIRO-B.

Chapter 8 - Genuine teamwork

For example:

- Too few extroverts can result in a lack of action and too much thought so that things do not move along quickly enough.
- Too few introverts can result in a rash of precipitate action without doing checks and balances.
- Too few intuitives can lead to the longer term and the bigger picture being ignored.
- Too few sensing people can lead to practical consequences not being dealt with.
- Too few value-based decision makers can create a hard-nosed uncaring approach.
- Too few logical decision makers can cause an avoidance of difficult people issues.
- Too few perceiving types can lead to rigidity and inflexibility.
- Too few judging types can lead to chaos and nothing being completed.
- A team full of people with low 'inclusion' will tend to work in a series of compartments.
- A team full of people with a high need for control will result in everyone fighting for space.
- A team full of people who are cautious about expressing 'affection' will feel that their colleagues are unappreciative of their efforts.

The process used for teams to understand themselves

The first step in the process is for each member in the team to complete Myers Briggs and Firo questionnaires and to receive individual one to one feedback on the results. It is vital that each individual understands and recognises their own profile before it is shared with anyone else. This feedback process needs to reinforce the positive benefits from the individual's profile and not to be overly concerned with any negative consequences. Using a profile properly and positively will minimise any negative effects.

The second step in the process is for a collective team session to be held during which each person's individual profile is outlined against the background of the MBTI® and Firo frameworks. Team members are able to discuss whether the person's behaviour always

Chapter 8 - Genuine teamwork

conforms to that description or not. If the session is well facilitated, the team will identify what it would like each individual to do more of, or less of, to aid the collective effect.

Two stages are then also possible. One is to consider the collective team profile and how this enables or hinders the team in securing its objectives. The other is to discuss issues relating to relationships with other teams which might work well or not so well and how this team's profile may be impacting on those relationships.

If there is a major problem between a team and another team, addressing it will require both teams to go through the above process to provide a platform for considering any problems between them. Resolving these would involve sharing the teams' profiles in a joint session with all members of both teams present.

Teamwork - senior management team

In examining teamwork we will start with potentially one of the most difficult teams in the organisation, the senior management team.

We use the term 'team' loosely since the constituent members of a team should have a common objective. In the case of senior management teams, these are often competitive battlegrounds for power, influence and succession. All the individuals within a senior management team will have reached this level because they are better than, or stronger than, their peers. Small wonder therefore that a battleground exists.

The trick is to value each member of the team for what they bring and to get each of them to value their colleagues likewise. In our experience this requires full individual understanding of each person's MBTI® and FIRO-B profiles and the sharing of this information in a positive and constructive environment. In some cases this can be a sensitive exercise to carry out. In our experience competition can be particularly prevalent in single sex management teams and can cause the individuals to be very wary about 'passing information to the opposition'. It is vital for the person facilitating the process to preserve as far as is appropriate the egos of each individual member.

The essence of this approach is to enhance understanding about the positive differences between individuals as a means of properly recognising the benefits they bring whilst

Chapter 8 - Genuine teamwork

endeavouring to prompt improvements to be made which benefit the organisation as a whole. Certain types of issues for instance may be given a lower priority than they should, or at worst, avoided completely because there is no one in the team who is comfortable with addressing them. Such gaps need to be filled in a different way for each team so that solutions are generated that fit the collection of individuals that are there, not a stylised team profile. At the end of the day, you still have that particular collection of people in that team. You may not have the luxury of changing the team.

Creating a degree of cohesion within this team creates important signals for the rest of the organisation. If you are trying to create a connected organisation the people at the top need to lead collectively by example otherwise everyone else may not follow. This should be seen against the often observed practice of encouraging competition for the role of successor to the Chief Executive, competition for available resources and competition relating to influencing the way the organisation is headed. Collaborative behaviour impacts positively on the bottom-line. In-fighting creates a negative impact.

Beware of detractors to this approach. Those who trumpet competitiveness to the exclusion of everything else are often the most competitive and the ones who are often interested in status for status's sake. The approach we advocate is not a mere technique, it is about recognising real people for what they are. Doing this well and endeavouring to combine their talents effectively is the best way of moving forward. Competition focuses on individuals and detracts from doing good for the benefit of everyone. At its worse competitive behaviour in the senior management team leads to warring behaviour in respective departments, wasted effort spent in undermining other departments and a failure to focus on the real issues challenging the organisation.

Teamwork - departmental management teams

The same principles and processes need also to be adopted for these teams as outlined above for senior management. The difference is that there can be more cohesion within departmental teams because the vast majority of team members come from the same professional or operational background. However this can also bring another set of disadvantages that can perhaps best be illustrated by some examples.

Chapter 8 - Genuine teamwork

Finance Department - a typical financial accountant will conform to a particular MBTI® profile. This is likely to be such that they follow the rules correctly, precisely and in the right order and expect to get everything 100% correct. If there is a preponderance of these in the team, the Finance Department may be seen as robust by the Auditors but picky, inflexible and unresponsive by the rest of the organisation. This is not to say that all financial teams are like this, or indeed that all accountants are like this, but there will be common tendencies because of the nature of the work involved. (N.B. In defence of those that follow the rules correctly etc... we have met examples who are very positive, embrace change and are willing to do things differently).

Marketing Department - marketing people tend to be driven by concepts which are often graphically represented, for example in advertising material. On occasions the product gets lost in the overall creativity of the advertisement. Marketing people tend to be full of strategic ideas, alternatives and possibilities. They can be seen by the more practical production oriented parts of the organisation as having their heads in the clouds and unable to make their minds up. The MBTI® profile that can be particularly prevalent here is the one that is innovative, flexible, stimulating, exciting and excitable. If so these people need clear direction and parameters as boundaries for their creativity.

Example 16 – A marketing company

A well known UK advertising agency quite naturally had a large number of creative and innovative people producing the next best ideas for advertisements. Hence it was very ideas-oriented. This organisation only survived by having an administrative lynch pin who ensured that the necessary and boring supporting tasks were undertaken. Otherwise the bills would not have been paid, the invoices would not have been sent out.

Production Department - production people tend to be practical realists who actively do things, make sure that they work and are results-oriented i.e. how many units have we made today. If so, stopping to consider changes in the way things are done may be frowned upon as will revolutionary ideas from marketing people who have no concept of the practical difficulties generated by their pronouncements.

Chapter 8 - Genuine teamwork

Within all departmental teams there will be some individuals who are different to the norm for their profession. The extent to which they are listened to may depend on what the differences are. Care needs to be taken that their views are not drowned out because they are not conforming to the normal way of looking at things. Organisations need to make sure that their views are heard and taken account of so that a fully rounded consideration takes place about the way forward.

Teamwork- project teams

Project teams are often the easiest to work with because they usually have a defined set of objectives and timescales. Following the team building process identified above at an early stage in the project will ensure that the team gets up to speed quickly and will increase the likelihood of it hitting its targets. This is especially important where project team members are drawn from different departments, or indeed, different organisations. Each may have their own cultures i.e. ways of doing things. They may or may not align. Actively addressing these differences as opposed to ignoring them will lead to positive performance benefits.

As a general starting point, having a mixture of individual profiles provides the most effective project team. Having mostly one particular profile (irrespective of what it is) may result in something akin to a ship jamming right rudder. If it needs to turn left that is very easy. If it needs to turn right it might need to exercise a 360 degree manoeuvre to do so. You need to remember that members of any team need to be selected first for their technical expertise and second for their fit, otherwise the people may not have the necessary skills to execute the task never mind the appropriate behavioural characteristics.

Teamwork- multi-disciplinary teams

Melding together multi-disciplinary teams is a complex process because the members usually come from a range of different organisations. They may have different value sets as well as different methods of working. They may all have different and conflicting interests and objectives. Creating a single cohesive approach becomes more problematic. Nonetheless starting with the process described above is the soundest means of

Chapter 8 - Genuine teamwork

proceeding. It may be that additional specific processes need to be added to clarify and manage these differences. Care needs to be taken that the representatives of each organisation remain the same individuals throughout the process. The sending of substitutes will change the consequent behavioural dynamics of the team with the result that cohesion built up will be dissipated or lost. An example of this can be seen in meetings between nations. These depend very much on who participates for their ultimate effectiveness.

Other team building techniques

The approach we are advocating in this chapter is designed to promote the understanding of team members about themselves and their colleagues. This understanding should act as a bedrock on which other team building activities can be built. The shared experiences of away days, abseiling, the Christmas Party and so forth all have their place in creating shared experiences within which team members interact with one another. It is the mutual understanding that underpins these that can make the biggest difference. However these other activities can help to sustain and reinforce the benefits over a long period.

Summary

The vast majority of people work in teams such as senior management teams, departmental (functional) teams, project teams, and multi-disciplinary teams. Many people work in several teams. For these to function effectively they each need to:

- Understand the contribution that each team member makes to the team and their individual personal style and approach.

- Understand the overall way in which the team approaches it's work.

- Understand the strengths, drawbacks and gaps within the team.

- Understand how each team relates to other teams.

- Use that understanding wisely and proactively within and between teams.

Chapter 8 - Genuine teamwork

Using the above approach should increase the cohesion within each team and between teams. This should lead to less wasted time, fewer unnecessary arguments and improved bottom-line performance.

Optimising this effect will only be achieved by having mutually understood communications which we turn to in the next Chapter.

Chapter 9 - Mutually understood communications

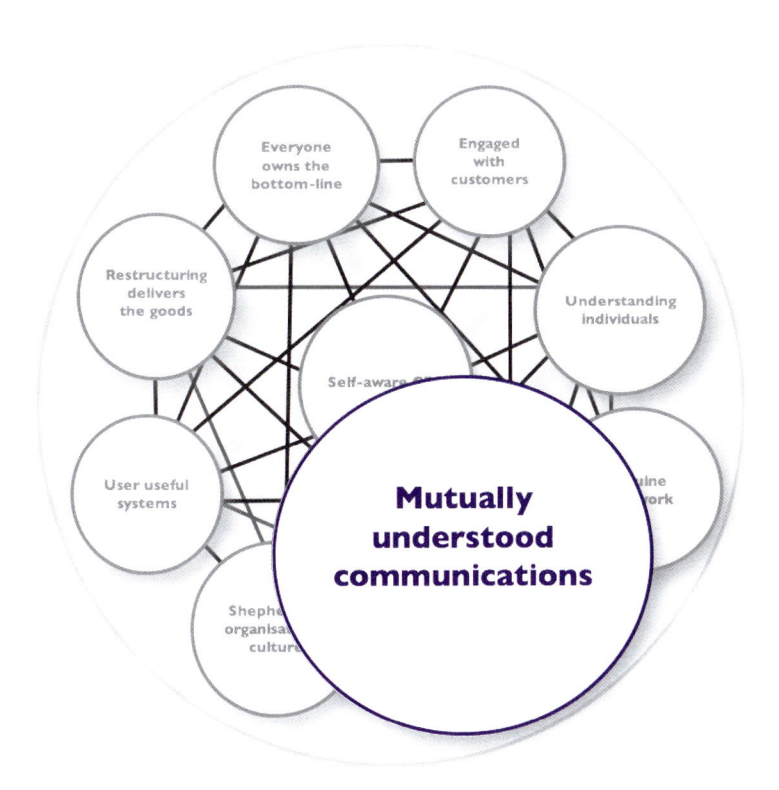

The issue

Everyone's innate nature means that they are good at half the elements of effectively interlinked communication. Each person needs to learn the other half to achieve mutually understood communications which in their very nature are two-way. Communication includes effective hearing, listening and understanding, not just a one way process of imparting information.

Connecting to the bottom-line

The importance of communications is to ensure that all people within an organisation know what they are about, why they are doing what they are doing, and who they need to communicate with about which things. Communication provides the connecting glue that holds the organisation together. To be effective, the flow in communications needs to be

Chapter 9 - Mutually understood communications

up and down and sideways. It needs constant refreshing lest the natural effect of the inevitable 'rumour mill' takes hold over actual reality.

In looking at communications we need to take into account two main facets:

- The processes involved, and
- The way in which individual people use and respond to these processes.

Please remember that communication by word of mouth is in itself a process. The speaker may assume that what they have said has been fully understood and if passed on by the recipient the same information will be imparted. This is not always the case. There is the famous quote from World War 1 where a message begins with "send reinforcements we are going to advance" and through mishearing and misquoting becomes "send three and fourpence we are going to a dance".

On the positive side, word of mouth communication enables immediate feedback to be obtained and understanding to be accurately checked. The implications of the information imparted can be considered and any subsequent action is enabled to happen as quickly as possible.

The most common form of business communication is now by emails, text messages, or other means of electronic communication. This is not by itself communication as it only represents half the process. You do not know whether it has been received, read, understood or acted upon accurately in accordance with the intention behind the message that was sent. Organising a 'read receipt' does not solve this problem. You still have to have feedback to know that the communication has worked or not.

The danger can be that you send out message after message assuming that the receiver is understanding what you have said and is acting on it as you would wish. Many people think that the mere sending of a message achieves a result. This is not the case until two-way communication has successfully taken place. When you get a reply you may still not have completed the process. The responder may have felt unable to give you a real answer for fear of upsetting you, or for a range of other reasons. You cannot see their face or judge their bodily reactions. 80% of human communication is non-verbal i.e. body

Chapter 9 - Mutually understood communications

language, facial expressions, attitudes and responsiveness. If you have this you will be much clearer on whether the person has understood, agrees with what has been said, and is going to act accordingly. Electronic communication on its own does not give you this information or feedback.

When emails didn't exist you had two choices to get a message across. You either spoke or wrote. Consequently communications were less frequent and better understood. Since emails have been used there has been an explosion of apparent communication which can waste large amounts of time to no great effect. People typically report spending an hour and a half at the beginning of the day reading and responding to emails. Much of this is a considerable cost over what used to happen in the past. We would seriously question whether there has been a commensurate increase in understanding and bottom line benefit.

In our experience people may be using emails to avoid the challenge of face to face contact with others.

> Example 17 – Why talk to someone when you can email them?
>
> In one organisation we worked in, a manager sent an email to instruct the person in the adjacent office to change the time of their lunch break. Needless to say the recipient was more than a little upset that the manager didn't just talk to them about it. They felt undervalued, ignored and personally slighted that the manager could not spare the small amount of effort to explain the situation face to face and check that it was OK. The manager had no information as to whether this change had been noted or, if it had, whether it would create difficulties for the individual. They may for instance have had an important meeting arranged in their lunch hour.

Using video conference or similar technological means can appear to give you a face to face conversation without the need to be in the same place. However you will not be experiencing the same environment and will not be picking up all the non-verbal clues. Anyone who has felt the 'atmosphere' when walking into a room will understand this point. Video conferencing and similar techniques have their uses in a widely dispersed organisation but are not a substitute for genuine face to face contact.

Chapter 9 - Mutually understood communications

If you have a very sound in depth working relationship with another individual it will matter far less what means of communication you use. This is because both you and the other person understand more about each other's likely response to a wide range of matters and you will both know more about the intentions behind those responses. However most electronic communications are not with someone with whom you have established this depth of relationship.

Based on our extensive experience of a wide range of organisations in both the public and private sector we can say that all organisations have issues and problems with communications. The consequence is not just people being 'off message' but a lack of understanding of what they need to do and how they need to respond, and a lack of knowledge at the top of the organisation of what is happening at the bottom. This leads to waste of time, duplication of effort, inappropriate effort and at worst a mismatch between what is needed and what is actually done. All of these cost you money. The bigger the organisation the more it will cost. The more geographically spread the organisation is, the more communications problems cost you.

You cannot delegate the communication of your thoughts.

This applies whether you are the CEO or a disgruntled employee. Effective communication must be two way and involves listening and checking understanding as much as talking and issuing instructions. There is a danger that people believe when they have said something that it has been heard and understood in the way that the person saying it meant it. Do not assume that this is the case

The key element of the communication model described below is precisely this, i.e. 'what did you understand by what I said?'

The Mobius Model

The following model, named after a Mobius strip (a continuous one-sided surface), identifies six elements to effective communication. It links these elements with individual's cognitive styles (the MBTI® type which is part of each individual's personality profile).

Chapter 9 - Mutually understood communications

Whatever your MBTI® type you are naturally inclined to perform only three of the six elements. The remaining three get assumed or are overlooked. It is small wonder that most organisations have communication problems.

The letters in the segments refer to the MBTI® (F is feeling, N is intuition, EJ is extrovert and judging, IP is introvert and perceiving, T is thinking, S is sensing, IJ is introvert and judging, and EP is extrovert and perceiving).

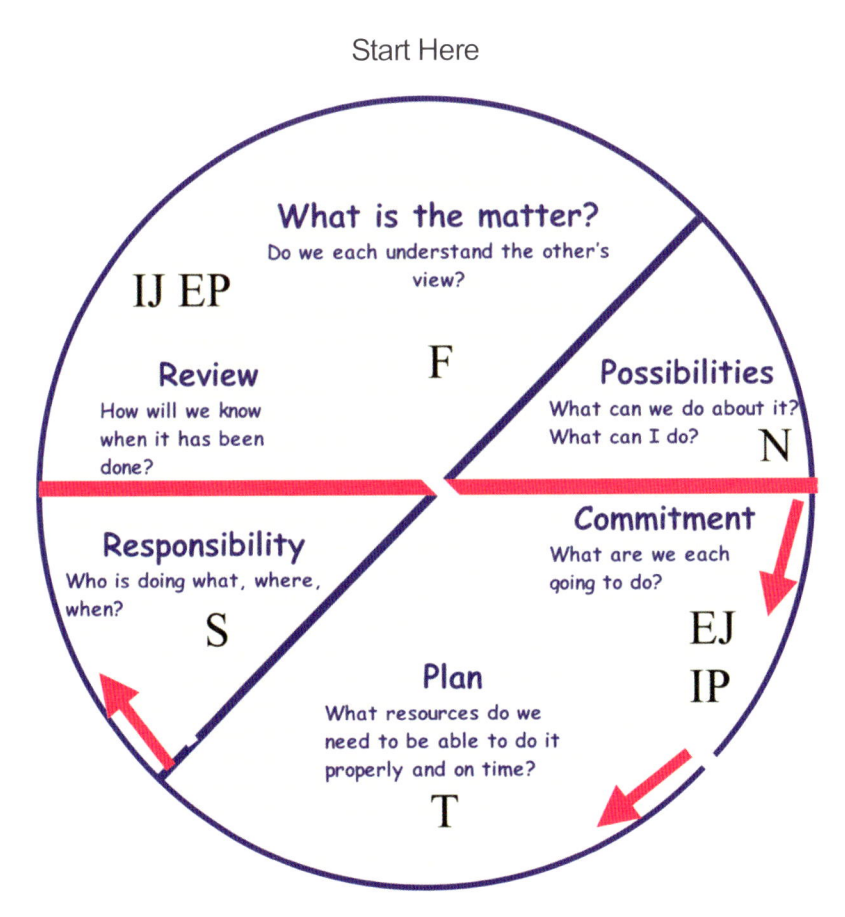

Start Here

IJ EP

What is the matter?
Do we each understand the other's view?

F

Review
How will we know when it has been done?

Possibilities
What can we do about it?
What can I do?

N

Responsibility
Who is doing what, where, when?

S

Commitment
What are we each going to do?

EJ
IP

Plan
What resources do we need to be able to do it properly and on time?

T

This model was originally built for the purpose of effective business conversations by two Americans, William Stockton and Marjorie Herdes (see www.mobiusmodel.com). In following the model you start by having some 'issue' i.e. a need to have a conversation.

Chapter 9 - Mutually understood communications

You first seek mutual understanding of the different positions of interested parties. You conclude by reviewing the actions taken to implement an agreed approach. Following this process for communications in general leads to effective implementation of what is required to address the issues and problems you started out with.

The mutual understanding element is the lynch pin of this model. If two or more people have different views each of them needs to explain to the other(s) what these are. The other(s) have to repeat them out aloud until their colleague says "you've got it". This sounds simple. What actually happens is that when each person does the repeating back they put their own 'spin' on it. They do not repeat what was said but what they 'heard'. Establishing mutual understanding (note: this does not require mutual agreement) is vital to successfully executing the rest of the process.

By making people go through the steps in the correct sequence and in the correct manner there should be no room for misunderstandings and no room to forget to execute any element of what is required. Should you, at the end of this process, have a residual issue you can address it by going through the steps for a second time, and possibly a third or fourth time if necessary.

This is by its nature a face to face communications process. It can be equally applicable to written communications provided that you anticipate correctly what the position and concerns of the recipients might be and allow for them to confirm or deny this and input to following parts of the process. We would argue that you need to have had direct experience of using the model on a face to face basis to understand what to do with it on a written basis.

For example if you were announcing a merger or acquisition you would first try to anticipate the key issues that your people might have on hearing the news - by placing yourself in their shoes. You may not at this point have answers for all of those issues. However you would need to think about how people might comment on them, consider any additional issues you hadn't initially thought about, identify how others might be involved in resolving them, and include time in the process for dealing with the issues. In such circumstances it might help you to refer to the section in Chapter 7 on 'Taking responsibility for collective treatment of individuals'.

Chapter 9 - Mutually understood communications

Other communication mechanisms

Two additional examples of helpful communication mechanisms are:

- The use of face to face question and answer sessions where the MD, a director or a senior manager is available to be questioned by anyone who turns up on any subject relevant to the business.
- The regular and timely production of written results of meetings to keep people apprised of progress.

With both of these, as with the Mobius model outlined above, it is not the following of the process that is the key to success. It is the way in which each part of the process is followed. So you need to say or write the right kind of things. If not, the people will fill in the blanks for themselves. Abraham Lincoln was right 'you can fool all the people some of the time, and some of the people all of the time, but you will never fool all of the people all of the time'.

The fact that we live in the so-called 'communication era' has introduced new methods of communication that if not properly managed can create unnecessary and counter-productive detachment between the sender and the recipient of the message with consequential damage to the bottom-line. The use of email in particular can be a method not of true communication but of avoidance of communication with the consequence of potential disagreement and even alienation of your people.

Emails are best used as confirmation, clarification and expansion of previous conversations. The stronger the relationship between the people involved, the more likely it is that email communication is effective. Badly managed, email communication sends a strong message that 'you are not important to me; I can't be bothered to talk with you by phone or face to face'.

Chapter 9 - Mutually understood communications

Example 18 – The grapevine always beats the formal process?

We carried out a consultancy exercise to reorganise 2,000 computer systems staff employed by a major clearing bank. Our proposals were accepted by management and a major venue was booked for the presentation of the results. The many hundreds of staff who attended this presentation said that they learned nothing as a result. The reason for the above sequence of events was that management had decided to take all the necessary decisions before communicating anything formally to the people affected. This included who was to get which job. What happened was that all the key players involved had had private conversations with the individuals to tell them whether they would be OK or not as a result of the reorganisation. Management had achieved a position of going all the way round the communication wheel by themselves. This made the resultant fanfare of trumpets a complete waste of time and money. Banking organisations naturally respond to the last three elements of the communications wheel. What's the plan, who's doing it and when is it going to be done by? People concerns are assumed, possible alternative courses of action ignored, and collective commitment is totally absent from the process. The consequences were the immediate costs of a loss of over 1,000 man days of work and the cost of hiring the hall. The other consequence was that management looked stupid.

Formal and informal communication mechanisms (managing the grapevine)

Whatever formal mechanisms are used for communications in your organisation there will be a parallel set of informal communications. These may be conversations in the corridor, the toilets, the dining room or the bar as friends and acquaintances exchange their reactions to past, current and potential future events. As a CEO or a senior manager you have no control over these processes but you do need to remember that they are there. On occasions, prompting the grapevine may enable you to get things into the system without any formal statements. Tapping into the grapevine may enable you to learn important things before they pass the point of no return.

People have a natural tendency to believe the grapevine rather than the official version. However much you say, there may be a belief that you are still hiding something. Ensuring that your official communications are accurate, regular and timely will be the best way of keeping in front of the grapevine. If you allow time gaps to occur or you miss out elements which other people can easily guess (rightly or wrongly) the grapevine will fill the void. So if

Chapter 9 - Mutually understood communications

you are not careful, paranoia will be alive and well in your organisation. If this gets into the market place you could be in some difficulty. Negative messages transmit at a higher speed than positive ones!

Summary

As we said at the beginning, in our experience all organisations have problems of communication. It is important therefore that energy is put into communication systems, and a level of responsiveness to events is adopted which stops time and resources being wasted and contributes to people being connected together with a shared and common understanding. Badly handled communication gives rise to a negative impact on your bottom-line. We have given you suggestions how you might reduce this.

To provide effective communications you need to:

- Understand the 6 elements of effective communication as described in the Mobius model above.
- Follow these steps in the correct sequence.
- Pay particular attention to step 1 (establishing mutual understanding - not agreement).
- Irrespective of your personal style, no-one is a fully effective communicator - this has to be continually worked on and feedback sought at every suitable opportunity.
- Recognise that electronic communication does not automatically work without other supporting processes.

Following the above will result in less time being wasted, greater harmony between parts of the organisation, and faster production of the right results.

We next turn to putting individuals, teams and communication into the context of the organisation's culture. Shepherding this effectively will give further enhancements in performance.

Chapter 10 - Shepherding organisational culture

(Diagram: Central circle "Shepherding organisational culture" surrounded by: Everyone owns the bottom-line; Engaged with customers; Understanding individuals; Genuine teamwork; Mutually understood communications; User useful systems; Restructuring delivers the goods; Self-aware CEO)

The issue

Organisational culture, 'the way we do things round here', is the normal behaviour adopted by the totality of the people in the organisation. They will have learned that this is the easiest way of coping with everything that needs to be done. The CEO can influence it but cannot determine it by decree. If aligned positively towards your bottom-line it will have a beneficial effect.

Organisational culture has a major impact on business performance. Actively shepherding it minimises energy being misspent on extraneous and non-productive activities. However, more often than not, culture happens by default rather than design. Whilst senior

Chapter 10 - Shepherding organisational culture

management set the overall direction, culture is created by the involvement of everyone not just by senior management on their own. "The way we do things around here" is about behaviours not about what is written down in procedure manuals and rule books.

If your organisation operates in more than one country, each has its own distinctive national culture. Organisations need to mesh their own culture with the cultures of the countries they operate within, and if needs be, to do things differently in different places. This Chapter tells you how to describe culture and provides indicators about doing things differently to achieve optimal success.

What do we mean by 'Culture?'

Culture consists of three distinctly separate elements, all of which interact with each other in determining what really happens:

1. Each country has its own culture.
2. Each organisation has its own culture.
3. Each team has its own culture.

Within this cocktail of culture each individual person has their own natural style and approach which they may amend, or not, to fit in with this mix.

Culture is the way we do things around here. This can have no connection whatsoever with written policies, procedures and instructions, since it depends on the collective appreciation by all those involved as to what constitutes survival or success. This is not the organisation's success, but what each individual regards as being success or failure for them.

When we walk into a business we immediately receive 'messages' about its culture. How is the visitor greeted? Do people address each other formally or informally? Are office doors open or shut? Is information shared or is knowledge power? How often do we hear 'our customer' mentioned? Do people relate their jobs to the bottom-line? Are there strong signals about ethics? How well do senior managers know other staff? Is there a sense of pride? Do people enjoy what they do? We can smell the culture - can you?

Chapter 10 - Shepherding organisational culture

Why is culture important?

It's not so much what your organisational culture is, but whether it aligns with what you are trying to do. If it gets in the way you need to know how it can be altered to obtain the effect you want. If the culture doesn't fit, your bottom-line results will not be as good as they should be.

The most appropriate word that describes what you as the CEO needs to do in respect of organisational culture is to 'shepherd' it in the direction you wish it to go. You can't take charge of culture as it is a collective thing. It does not respond to simple instructions but it can be influenced if concerted action is taken up by sufficient people. If you are the CEO the issue is how to influence such change in the most effective way. When you, as CEO, issue instructions you may not appreciate the other actions that are generated on an automatic basis by the organisation's culture. You need to remember, in particular if you are a new CEO, that the former CEO's ways of doing things will have been taken into account in the way people behave. Your's are likely to be different. The previous CEO may not have been fully aware of their own impact and the chances are you might not learn fully what your's is. People have a habit of not telling CEOs about things that might be viewed as detrimental to their interests.

Your actions might therefore be said to have a similar effect to Heisenberg's 'Uncertainty Principle'. In simple terms this states that when viewing an electron you are not actually looking at the electron but where it was. Your actions have moved it elsewhere to an uncertain position. Your attempts to influence the organisation can have a similar effect.

If your organisation operates in a number of different countries you need to remember that each of these has a different culture. This is perhaps most simply encapsulated by the phrase "when in Rome, do as the Romans do". You need to pay attention to the different ways of doing things 'round here'. Doing so will increase the level of effectiveness achieved and the resultant profits which the organisation may enjoy.

Chapter 10 - Shepherding organisational culture

Identifying what the culture is

There are two means of doing this we are familiar with and are happy to recommend to others.

One is the 'Cultural Web' developed by Gerry Johnson, Professor of Strategic Management at Cranfield School of Management, and Kevan Scholes, Professor of Strategic Management at Sheffield Business School, who wrote a book "Exploring Corporate Strategy" (Prentice Hall 1989). This deals with the culture within an organisation.

The second means is the Myers Briggs Type Indicator (MBTI®) referred to earlier. This has been used to describe the culture within an organisation through a book written by William Bridges "The Character of Organisations" (Consulting Psychologists' Press Inc.1992). The same instrument can also be used to describe the culture of a country.

These instruments can be used together as they focus on slightly different aspects of the organisation and hence provide a richer picture than that obtained by using either in isolation.

The Cultural Web

The model developed by Johnson and Scholes consists of seven inter-related circles as shown overleaf.

Chapter 10 - Shepherding organisational culture

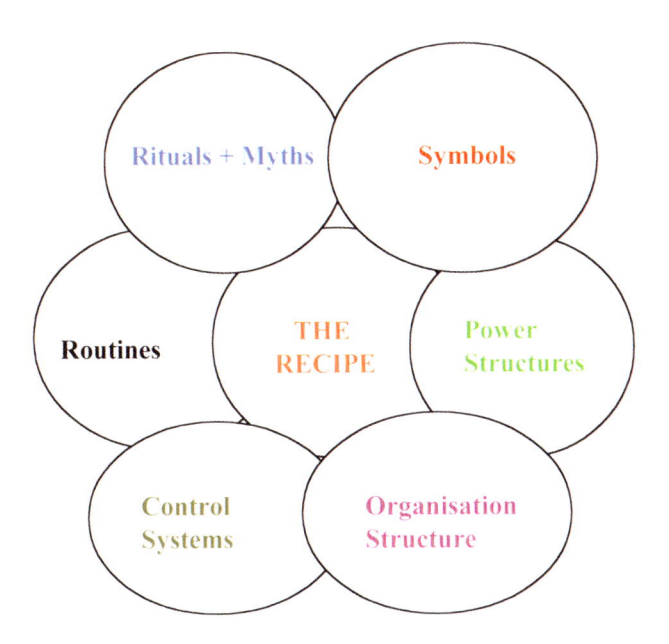

From Johnson & Scholes: Corporate Strategy

The three circles comprising, **organisational structures, control systems, and routines** will be familiar to anyone from an organisational working environment. These are the ones that organisations change whenever they embark on any kind of change process.

The three circles comprising **rituals + myths, symbols, and power structures** receive little, if any, attention. What are they?

Symbols are things such as named executive car park spaces, key to an executive toilet, the size of executive offices, separate senior management dining room, whether you have a secretary or not, and so on. They are the things that symbolise something of importance to individuals or groups in a particular organisation.

Rituals + myths include stories of what happened in the past, what happens about mistakes, what happens when things are done well, rituals of indoctrination, rituals of how

Chapter 10 - Shepherding organisational culture

you relate to senior executives. None of these will be written down. They are passed on by word of mouth from person to person and can act as major constraints on progress.

Power structures are nothing to do with formalised organisation structures. They could be the caretaker in a school who holds sway over everything. They can be to do with the background of the person concerned - are they from the right school or university (alumni), are they from the right profession? Certain people are listened to more than others for potentially inappropriate reasons.

Collectively these three parts of the system represent what might be called the 'informal organisation'. They can have a restraining effect on the organisation's performance, and more particularly on its ability to change.

The seventh and central element is called '**The Recipe**'. This is a summary of the key parts of what the organisation is about. For example, taking a manufacturing company, it could read something like this - reliability, product performance, after sales service, customer loyalty, and importance of experience.

The reason that organisation culture can have a negative influence is because it evolves more by accident than by design. It exists because it provides safety and certainty to the people in the organisation about what happens.

How do we manage culture using the 'Cultural Web'?

In change processes organisations pay attention to, attend to and amend organisation structures, control systems and routines. In order to secure effective and sustained change, the other three elements, Rituals + Myths, Symbols and Power Structures need to be assessed and aligned. If the change process is a fundamental one the Central Recipe may also need to change.

Changing Rituals + Myths, Symbols and Power Structures cannot be dealt with by simple managerial instructions. They require the compliance and support of the workforce as a whole. There needs to be agreement and preferably consensus both on what happens now and on what changes can be made. It is also essential that feedback is obtained as

Chapter 10 - Shepherding organisational culture

the change process takes place to see that these elements of the cultural web are indeed moving to where they need to be, and that there are no lapses into old style cultural behaviours. Just using your managers to do this will not achieve success; the rest of the workforce needs to be comfortable that behavioural changes will be made by everyone. In particular, the stories generated along the way will be the result of private conversations between individual members of staff which then get spread around by the organisational grapevine. You will need to find a way of tapping into this grapevine to secure success.

Perhaps the most crucial factor in achieving cultural change is the extent to which you, as the CEO, 'model' whatever the new way is of doing things. If you do not reinforce the changes you are making, the signal you will be giving is that the change is not important to you. If so, why on earth should it be important to anyone else?

Using the MBTI® to describe and manage culture

The MBTI® can be used to look at culture at three levels.

- The country the organisation is based in.
- The organisation itself.
- The organisation's constituent teams – as described in Chapter 8.

If your organisation is a multinational company do not assume that your culture is consistent in all the countries in which you operate. You may want it to be so, but if your organisational culture is at odds with the culture of a particular country you may not be able to operate the same way in that country. It may be a global marketplace but it is not a homogenous one.

We have already talked about the use of the MBTI® in identifying individual's styles and approaches and those of teams. William Bridges, in his book referred to above, describes amongst other things whether an organisation is inward or outward looking and whether it looks to the future or the present. It also describes whether decision making is driven by logic or personal values and whether the organisation is ordered and planned or flexible and spontaneous. Whatever the answer, this can be related to where the organisation is

Chapter 10 - Shepherding organisational culture

trying to get to. You can then determine whether it enhances or detracts from the process of getting there.

This will identify what it is you may need to try and change about the organisation's culture to align it with achieving the required outcome.

> *Example 19 – Identifying an organisation's culture using MBTI®*
>
> *We issued the William Bridges questionnaire to all the senior executives in a major insurance company in Poland. The answers obtained showed at that time an internally focused organisation which dealt with today's problem in the slickest and easiest way possible. Little attention was paid to the external market place, to developing a cohesive and sustainable long term strategy and there was a lack of care evidenced towards both individual employees and individual customers. Remaining in this cultural state was not a sustainable long term option. Hence projects were put in place to ensure that the company's culture evolved into one which was better suited to the long term health and profit base of the organisation. Whilst the company intuitively felt that it had a problem, it was only by using this technique that it was able to accurately describe and begin to address what it was.*

Sometimes there may be an argument for not changing an organisation's culture but instead setting up a separate company to achieve a quite different objective. For instance a retail banking organisation could set up a venture capital company to support innovative new businesses rather than trying to weld such an operation into what may be a risk-averse base culture.

This brings us to the question of the culture of countries. We all know that the French do things differently to the Germans, to the Egyptians, the Indians, the Chinese, the Americans and the English. Why then if you are running a global organisation should you expect things to happen the same way in all of these places? Far better to attune what you do to the particular country in question. Is this not at the end of the day part of engaging with your customers and your people?

To illustrate the differences in the culture of countries we cite the following examples:

Chapter 10 - Shepherding organisational culture

Example 20 – Ignoring the impact of country culture

We were approached by a blue chip UK organisation that had a business partnership in the UK with a computer systems firm. They had recently set up a similar arrangement in Poland. It was not working. Our first question was - "before you embarked on this venture did you investigate what the Polish culture is?" "No" came the reply.

On further investigation there were clearly some distinct differences between the two cultures. On setting up these organisational arrangements, effort was diverted from achieving necessary business results because of a failure to recognise the way in which Polish people approach things. These differences are not huge but cause significant delay and lead to inappropriate actions being taken. The local Polish view can be that, at worst, the incoming companies have no idea what they are doing. This destroys confidence in senior management.

With our help these difficulties were resolved through discussion and the creation of mutual understanding. If the differences had been identified in the first place the business launch would have been more successful and completed in a shorter time.

Example 21 – Working with rather than against the country culture

The Japanese operations of a multi-national organisation we had dealings with had a number of issues relating to differences of country culture. At its simplest Japanese staff would not leave the office until after the CEO had left. When the CEO needed to stay late he had to formally leave the office and return at a later time - otherwise everyone else would have stayed. At a more complex level was a tendency of expatriate staff to get hung up trying to make local staff adhere to the processes extant in the parent company's home country.

This latter problem was overcome by changing the focus away from process and onto outcomes. In this way everyone could agree what had to be delivered. They could then discuss the best way of doing this.

Chapter 10 - Shepherding organisational culture

> *Example 22 – Different cultures working together*
>
> *An Australian MD had recently taken over as leader of a UK management team. The team were not performing in accordance with his expectations and he was having difficulty getting them to do what he wanted them to do. A team building session was held which included an assessment and discussion of the differences between UK and Australian culture using the MBTI®. The MD was surprised that UK culture was almost the opposite of Australian culture. The former was based on status and role and only changing what you are doing with permission. The latter was based on individuals solving problems on their own initiative and if it can't be done one way to do it another.*
>
> *It was necessary to work on bridging the gap between the two approaches to bring the team's actions closer to the MD's expectations. This is something which cannot be achieved in a single step.*

American culture is often said to be quite close to English culture. The preference for procedures, systems, signs and notices is quite apparent in both countries. However the way these are used is quite different. American culture is extroverted and hence active steps are taken to follow procedures. These actions are often very visible. English culture on the other hand is more introverted and the actions are therefore less visible and followed at a more sedate pace. These two cultures have different impacts on individuals.

> *Example 23 – The impact of culture on an individual*
>
> *We were told the following story by an American individual. When she was brought up, she was always being told to speak up and say what she meant i.e. to be extroverted in line with American culture. Often she found this uncomfortable, as she was a natural introvert and hence preferred quiet introspection. Her MBTI® type does not sit easily with the normal American way of doing things.*
>
> *If she had been English, her introverted nature would not have been regarded in itself as unusual. She might have been labelled as 'quiet' but other than that there would be no pressure from being an introvert in a naturally introverted culture. Were she loud and raucous then that would have been an issue.*

Chapter 10 - Shepherding organisational culture

Influencing and changing culture

You must appreciate that no one individual by themselves, no matter how powerful they are, can create a new culture. Everyone who works for the organisation is part of that culture. An inclusive process in one form or another needs to be used to develop and to sustain the change. Using the kinds of techniques we have identified provides some terminology for this process and helps everyone to identify what needs to be changed. They can then develop ideas as to how to address those needs with an understanding of the level of difficulty that may be experienced in following them through. Gaining ownership of what needs to be done from everyone is essential to moving forward so that new and modified behaviours can be integrated into normal ways of working. It is important to have checks and milestones along the way. It is also essential to ensure that the involvement you start with is continued. This forms the basis for successful achievement in a culture change process.

It should, by this point, be clear that any culture change needs to be one that encourages cohesion between the various parts of the organisation and is one that increases bottom-line results. A culture change process that is embarked upon merely for its own sake will not succeed in a sustained way.

Example 24 – Reinforcing culture

A global company we worked with gave its managers the freedom to adjust the way they operated to conform to local country culture in which they operated. At the same time they maintained a central development facility to ensure that the overarching values of the company were also transmitted consistently to managers throughout the group. This achieved an effective balance between the needs of the corporate organisation and its operations in countries with different cultures.

Chapter 10 - Shepherding organisational culture

Summary

Culture involves everybody. It is not determined by the CEO. Changing culture requires

- Involvement of all the people in the organisation.

- An idea of the culture you think you want which will support the needs of the organisation.

- A concerted programme which ensures that you and everyone else understand the behaviours that currently take place, why they occur and what the means are to change this.

The nature of your culture has a significant impact on the organisation's bottom-line. You need to shepherd it to ensure that this is a positive impact. The culture will not then get in the way of achieving business results.

In the next Chapter we look at the impact of systems and whether they reinforce or detract from all the things we have so far described in this book.

Chapter 11 - User useful systems

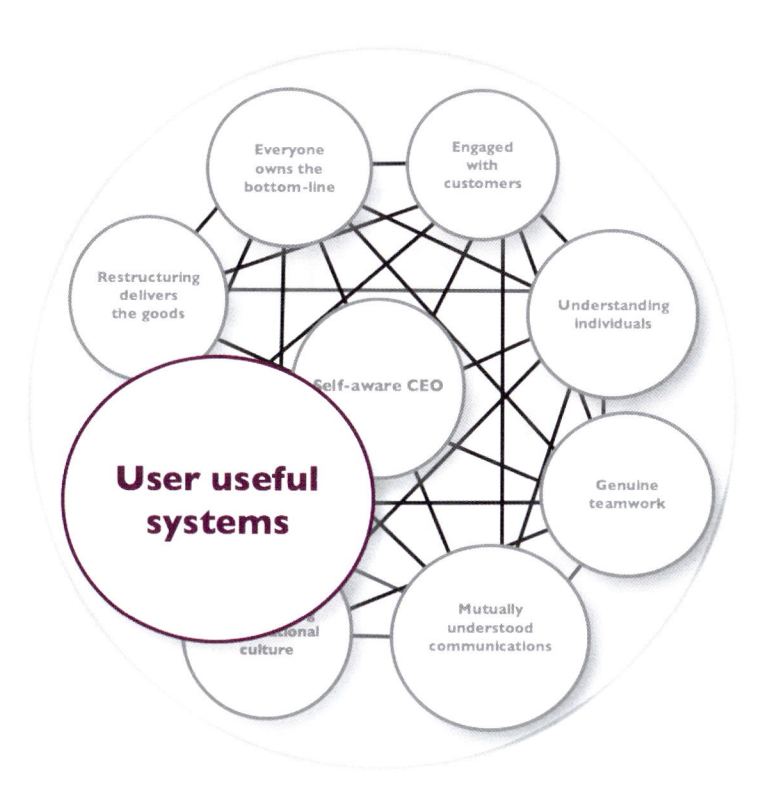

[Diagram showing "User useful systems" connected to surrounding concepts: Everyone owns the bottom-line, Engaged with customers, Understanding individuals, Genuine teamwork, Mutually understood communications, ...onal culture, Restructuring delivers the goods, and Self-aware CEO in the centre.]

The issue

Both manual and computerised systems need to be designed to actively meet the needs of users in achieving the organisation's objectives. They do not have a purpose of their own in isolation from these objectives.

By its nature, Information Technology is one of the key connectivity mechanisms within organisations and with clients. If properly managed and used it adds substantially to bottom-line results. It can be complex, technical and expensive and from our experience it can be a divisive influence and one that causes a great deal of negative reaction. In this chapter we discuss a number of issues related to the impact of Information Technology on connectivity within organisations and how to ensure that positive rather than negative results ensue.

Chapter 11 - User useful systems

The three issues we discuss are:

- Senior management understanding of IT and its influence on what does and doesn't happen.
- The dangers of assuming that computers are always right.
- Establishing and maintaining effective understanding between IT people and everyone else in the organisation.

N.B. the same issues will also apply to manual systems but in our experience these are generally less of a problem than ones that are technologically based. This is because the underlying structures of manual systems are usually more visible to everyone and more easily understood than technological ones.

Senior management understanding of IT

In many instances senior managers do not directly use the IT systems within the organisation (we are not talking about email). It is important for all senior managers to understand the limits and levels of accuracy of the information held on the main IT systems. For example does the financial system report only past expenditure or does it include future spending commitments or projections? Does the HR system include people who have been appointed and not yet started and does it retain leavers after they have left. Recognising these types of points will help you to understand the information presented from these areas such as whether we are within budget? Or, how many people do we have? This is part of understanding what a system can provide and what you must find out from elsewhere.

As mentioned in a previous chapter, numbers should be analysed together with the associated qualitative data. This almost certainly includes the parameters used to procure them and the limitations on accuracy and relevance of data.

Do you as a senior manager understand how each of the key IT systems within your organisation works, the nature of the technology and how up to date it is? You do not need to know the detailed technicalities but have sufficient knowledge to act as a basis for when judgements need to be made about changing or upgrading hardware, software or the

Chapter 11 - User useful systems

network. Without this understanding you have effectively abdicated the decisions to the IT specialists. You could be in danger of taking on board inappropriate technology, more than you need, or technology that doesn't deliver what the organisation requires at the time it needs it. Most businesses have IT as a major tool to aid in the functioning of the business. If it is that major you need to know about it. This is even more important if you have outsourced all or part of your IT to an external supplier.

Assuming the computer is always right

This can be illustrated by the following example that happened to one of us:

Example 25 – Computer information is only as accurate as the input that created it

One of us bought a motor car and contacted their insurance company to change their insurance. The insurance company employee said that according to their computer the car did not exist. However it did because it had just been purchased. What the insurance company was actually saying was that the particular make and model had not been included on the list on their computer system. The correct approach at this point would be to consult the appropriate underwriter about what course of action should be followed. However there is often an assumption that the computer system, not the client, is correct.

The above example clearly illustrates that computer systems only hold the information that is put into them. This function is carried out by human beings. If someone doesn't update the system the information on the computer will be wrong.

This assumption that information must be correct because it is on the computer system can make dealing with government agencies particularly challenging. These organisations, as well as many in the private sector, are not well reputed for correcting their mistakes. Once a piece of information has been entered the system, the impression is that no-one believes what you are saying is true and that no-one is authorised to correct it.

Another frustrating issue is when the customer phones up an organisation and is told, "we can't serve you because the computer is down". Why not? This kind of response suggests that all decisions and judgements have been abdicated to a machine. A back-up process

Chapter 11 - User useful systems

ought to be in place and people should be able, and permitted, to use their own judgement when something is obviously wrong.

To address these issues you have to empower your people to question the system and take appropriate action. You should also have a feedback system providing you with information on how often it is happening. If you do, your staff and your customers will have confidence in your organisation's record keeping. This will enhance your reputation with customers and make it more likely that they will continue to use your products and services.

Establishing and maintaining effective understanding between IT and users

IT people complain that users do not understand IT. Users complain that IT people do not understand their needs. What usually happens in these situations is that IT people find it difficult to explain what IT systems do in a language that is understood by their users. The users therefore have a less than clear understanding of what information technology can do to meet their needs. If they know the full potential of the technology it may help them clarify what their real needs are. They may realise that they have actual needs they hadn't thought of.

Attempting to resolve these difficulties by requiring users to specify their needs and IT departments to respond is a little like asking a Mandarin speaker to talk to a Russian speaker. The necessary processes need to be carried out jointly so that the IT people can learn what the users think they are trying to achieve and so that the users can be shown some of the potential the technology has. You should also remember that with certain systems e.g. the finance system, there are more than one set of users.

This process becomes more difficult if your IT has been outsourced. The IT organisation in this case has an inbuilt incentive to sell you what they think is the best thing ever, whether you need it or not. You may be able to manage with less which will cost you less. This might mean that you need to create a different mechanism for bridging the gap in understanding to find the solutions that are the best value for money.

Chapter 11 - User useful systems

A lot of the problems here are associated with difficulties in communication. We would refer the reader to Chapter 9 on to how to address these difficulties.

Example 26 – Beware the claims of IT suppliers

When seeking a new fully integrated Payroll/Personnel system for more than 20,000 employees a major computer supplier was contacted about whether they could supply an integrated system. The answer was yes. When asked to describe it, the supplier had separate personnel and payroll files and one of these was updated by the other every 24 hours. This meant that if two people interrogated two parts of the system at the same time on the same day they could receive two entirely different answers. This was not an integrated system and the supplier was not chosen.

This book is about turning organisations into cohesive entities. Your IT Department or supplier needs to be an integral part of this. You may need alterations in systems to take place to increase cohesiveness and IT staff need to understand both what is needed and why. Their active involvement should secure these objectives.

IT staff need to own the bottom-line, not just be used as a back room function. They also need to know what is happening in the market place and most importantly what you are trying to deliver to your customers. They can then best advise you on how the technology might best fit your customer value proposition.

Summary

Your IT operation should not be in a position of isolation within the organisation even when it is outsourced. As an integral part of how your organisation functions you should be ensuring the following:

- You understand in principle what your organisation's IT systems do, what the limitations are on the accuracy and completeness of the information they hold and where you might get any further complementary information.

Chapter 11 - User useful systems

- Ensure your staff do not adopt an attitude that the computer must always be right and are encouraged to check and act on any gaps in information or provision of services.
- Ensure that your IT department/supplier and the users have an active means of sharing information needs and how to meet them such that any issues are dealt with on a joint cooperative basis and not as two sides firing bullets at each other.
- IT staff need to be an integral part of moving the organisation forward.

Implementing the above should lead to effective IT operations that enhance the efficiency, effectiveness and bottom-line results of your business.

In the next Chapter we turn to what happens with restructuring and mergers and acquisitions, all of which have the potential to destroy as well as reinforce the cohesiveness described by following everything we have said in this book.

Chapter 12 - Restructuring delivers the goods

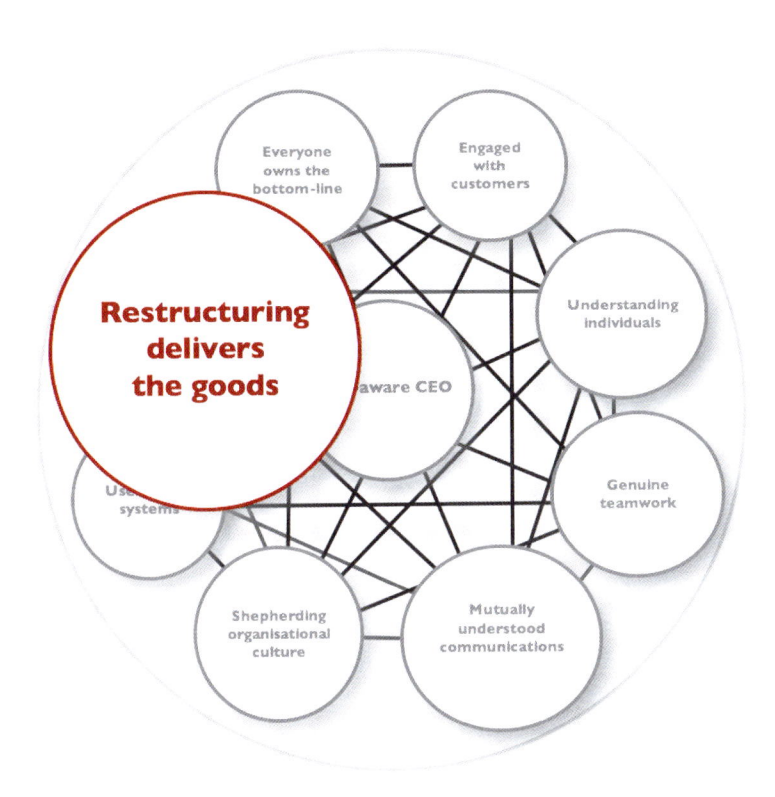

Diagram showing interconnected circles with "Restructuring delivers the goods" highlighted, surrounded by: Everyone owns the bottom-line, Engaged with customers, Understanding individuals, Genuine teamwork, Mutually understood communications, Shepherding organisational culture, Used systems, and aware CEO.

The issue

Most restructurings (including mergers and acquisitions) are undertaken to achieve improvements to service and bottom-line performance. Over many years actual results and academic research have shown however that a majority of these restructurings fail to achieve their anticipated benefits. This is due to an over concentration on the apparent positive benefits whilst ignoring or paying insufficient attention to managing the negative consequences. The original objectives used to justify the action in the first place are then not met.

This chapter will discuss what else you need to focus on, drawing on previously developed insights about the 'personalities' of teams and of different organisations and how these

Chapter 12 - Restructuring delivers the goods

interact. Such understanding significantly improves the quality of decision making and constructive management of these major organisation changes.

A value destroying process?

In 1987, Harvard Professor Michael Porter observed that between 50% and 60% of acquisitions were failures. In 1995 Mercer Management Consulting noted that between 1984 and 1994, 60% of the firms in the "Business Week 500" that had made a major acquisition were less profitable than their industry average. In 2004, McKinsey calculated that only 23% of acquisitions have a positive return on investment. Academic research in strategy and business economics have taken these conclusions further, suggesting that acquisitions destroy value for the acquiring firm's shareholders, although they create value for the shareholders of the target firm, something that was confirmed by a study carried out by the Boston Consulting Group (2007).

In 2007 a study by the Hay Group and the University of Paris identified that 90% of mergers in Europe failed to meet their financial goals. Separate research also indicates that there may be a large degree of corporate blindness, or a worrying refusal to acknowledge reality, in recognising poor outcomes:

Robert W. Holthausen, The Nomura Securities Company Professor, Professor of Accounting and Finance and Management stated:

> "83 percent of all mergers fail to create value and half actually destroy value. This is an abysmal record. What is particularly amazing is that in polling the boards of the companies involved in those same mergers, over 80 percent of the board members thought their acquisitions had created value."

Example 27 – Value destruction

In December 2009 the media conglomerate Time Warner spun off its America On Line (AOL) unit. Nine years previously it had acquired AOL the internet company for US$ 163 billion. The value of AOL at the time it was spun off had plummeted to approximately US$ 3.5 billion - a destruction of 98% of the price paid for AOL.

Chapter 12 - Restructuring delivers the goods

Time Warner/AOL is an extreme case attributed to the impact of the cultural mismatch of the two merging businesses. Whilst other merging activities may not have such catastrophic impacts on value there is ample evidence that the majority of them are failures.

This is all too often replicated in the Public Sector which has a predilection for using reorganisations as the solution to every problem.

> *Example 28 – Reorganising for the sake of it?*
>
> *In the UK, Child Care Service Departments (previously under the control of Social Services) were in recent years combined with Education Departments to create Departments of Children's Services. The purpose of this was to increase the degree of coordination between the departments concerned - especially in relation to vulnerable children. The size of the Education Service is vastly greater than that of Child Care Services for vulnerable children, and the cultures of these two operations is substantially different. They do not therefore make easy bedfellows in a single management structure. Changing the structure did not result in the anticipated improvements, evidenced by a further change now being introduced to Child Care Services as this book is being written.*

It is interesting to note that since Social Services Departments were first created in the 1970s they have been reorganised several times over and have been subject to numerous national studies and initiatives. Merely restructuring the organisation does not in itself deal with the core problem.

It has also been academically measured, that in internal reorganisation processes, productive output falls by 15% - 20% until the people issues have been resolved - often the difference between bottom-line profit and loss. This is a consequence of the managerial and investigative effort involved in setting up whatever the solution is and the diversion of everyone's attention to what is going to happen to them as a consequence. There will be innumerable informal discussions far outweighing the number of formal ones. The consequent danger is that everyone's eyes are taking off the ball of 'continuing to run business as usual'. Until people's positions are resolved to their satisfaction they may not

Chapter 12 - Restructuring delivers the goods

be as motivated as usual to carry out their role. The ultimate danger is the bottom-line is put on hold while the outcome of various negotiations are awaited.

In all of these circumstances one might wonder why on earth any organisation would take the risk of becoming involved in mergers, acquisitions or restructurings! The chances are that they will seriously damage the bottom-line.

Securing the right outcomes

In broad terms carrying out mergers, acquisitions and restructurings should have six key stages:

- An initial evaluation stage to decide why it is necessary to put effort into merging, acquiring or restructuring rather than into the organic development of the organisation.

- Identification and evaluation of suitable partners and/or structures and the economic or service value that should be achieved.

- Due diligence (in depth investigation) to ensure you know who and what you are getting (you need to include people assessment in this part of the process).

- Assessment of the similarities or differences in organisational culture.

- Identification of key people and system issues which may have a significant impact on implementation.

- An implementation process that moves the new structures forward to achieve the identified bottom-line goals.

It is not our purpose here to examine the technical aspects of these activities. We assume that any organisation undertaking mergers, acquisitions and restructurings will have more than adequate access to this form of advice and input. We are, however, conscious that the track record indicates beyond dispute that good technical advice does not of itself achieve good value outcomes. It points you in the right direction of the goals to be achieved but does not deliver them.

Chapter 12 - Restructuring delivers the goods

What we will concentrate on are the people aspects which will determine whether the enterprise is successful or not in carrying through the acquisition, merger or restructuring given that the financial indicators give the right justification. There are four core elements that we will focus on. These are:

- Assessing and reconciling different cultures.
- Aligning and connecting the people involved.
- Informing and responding to clients.
- Resolving IT systems differences.

All of these involve people. You cannot deal with any of them without dealing with the people involved. The higher level assessment of these elements will have been taken as part of the six key stages outlined above.

Assessing and reconciling different cultures

Organisational culture is a blend of an organisation's values, traditions, beliefs and priorities. Also, it helps determine and legitimise what sort of behaviour is rewarded in an organisation. Combining cultures requires a focus on one new vision and one new mission, developed by a cross-section team of representatives from both organisations. Problems typically occur when the larger or stronger of the two organisations tries to significantly influence the integration to the exclusion of the smaller or weaker one.

During the merger and acquisition process, the different cultures should be assessed, as should the likelihood of successfully combining them. This is a major risk to the future success of the business and should not be lightly passed over. It therefore should be an integral part of due diligence. If the cultures cannot be successfully reconciled the merger should not proceed. You are setting yourself up to fail.

Senior management must facilitate the birth of a new or modified culture by inspiring a new vision. This can be an impossible task without listening to the concerns of people at all levels through the process. In Chapter 10 we discussed organisational culture. In a merging situation you have to design a process that enables a newly merged culture to evolve over time. In our experience very little time and attention is paid to such processes

Chapter 12 - Restructuring delivers the goods

in comparison to what is required to meet the need. This can ultimately lead to a merger failing at worst. Alternatively existing cultures remain in place for a long time after the merger and continue to be a source of division and wasted effort. This may not affect the chief executive directly but will substantially impact on the bottom-line. The CEO needs to make sure that cultural problems are not preventing the 'new organisation' from moving on.

There is no standard way of merging two cultures because all cultures are different. How to do it depends on the nature of the differences and the expectations of the two groups of people involved. Chapter 10 describes how you would start, but how you progress from there needs to be individually tailored according to circumstance. It is important to recognise that the final culture will be different to that of either of the original merging organisations.

Aligning and connecting people

When you acquire or merge businesses you are in reality acquiring or merging people. When you are restructuring you are shuffling people about. Everything that happens in business is a consequence of what people do. In situations where businesses are combining it is in effect people who are combining.

In any two businesses the way that people have worked together, the systems and procedures they have used, the organisation culture, the management styles used will all have been quite different. It cannot be assumed that simply making people work together will somehow resolve the differences. Indeed it is far more likely to increase tensions and undermine cooperation and productivity.

> A Forbes survey of 500 Chief Financial Officers found that the top reasons why mergers failed were not financial issues, but people-related issues: incompatible cultures, inability to manage the acquired company, inability to implement change, synergy* overestimated, failure to forecast foreseeable events, or clashing management styles or egos.

Chapter 12 - Restructuring delivers the goods

* positive synergy is where the whole is greater than the sum of the constituent parts.

To deal with these issues you need to have a well considered people strategy ready for immediate implementation once a merger or acquisition is announced. The first thing people want to hear is not what is happening to the company or the organisation, it is what is happening to **them**. You may not have all the answers at this point but you must have a clear philosophy and process so people can judge when they will know and how they might secure their future to best possible effect.

The key drivers for the change and the organisational benefits will serve to increase or decrease the level of aggravation amongst the people involved according to whether it makes sense to them or not. If you have aggravation, you have to be willing to find out why, and to then be willing to discuss and respond to the issues that have emerged. This will not necessarily convert other people to your perspective but it will increase their confidence that the process is being handled properly. Remember from Chapter 7, if you respect and involve your workforce in the business they will support and enhance what you are trying to do.

At the outset the issue of top level appointments is not only critical to organisational success but automatically gives out messages to the rest of the workforce. You should resist the temptation to simply accommodate people for convenience. This is the moment when you need to recognise that you need the right people in the right places. Otherwise the whole process will fail. You need an actively managed and inclusive process of those people in the merging organisations who might be seen as potential contenders that enables appropriately qualified and experienced people to be considered properly for the top level jobs. This will often have to occur ahead of the public announcement of the acquisition or merger. Merely allocating a job on the basis of previous status, or whether they are someone's colleague, is not a good foundation for future progress and success. We would refer you to the comprehensive selection processes outlined in Chapter 7 and in particular to the benefit of using independent external input. By using such people to ensure the best appointments are made, it increase the likelihood that everyone will accept that the outcomes are fair.

Chapter 12 - Restructuring delivers the goods

When one business acquires another, with the aim of creating something better out of the process, it is not the 'same' business that emerges. What emerges is something quite new with different strategies and different ways of working. If this was not the case then it would be pointless to go through the acquisition process - it would not be adding value.

The Board therefore needs to ask itself what sort of person is needed to successfully add value in the new circumstances being created. This is a vital decision that will effect all others. Difficult though it may be it is not always the correct decision to take the short cut and appoint the existing CEO into the new role. It is an opportunity to assess, preferably with independent support, what capabilities are required to achieve the outcomes assumed in justifying the acquisition. Are these similar to what has been required in the past or have elements of the business and its focus changed and therefore require new leadership styles?

Acquiring companies need to be aware of a "conquering army mentality". If one company is acquiring another, there needs to be some realization that the employees of the target company make it what it is and it may be more important to retain them than employees of the acquiring company. Either way if you appoint a preponderance of people from one organisation you are likely to generate a climate amongst the rest that they feel that they have been defeated.

You need to be aware that those people who stay will feel fortunate and will prefer it if those leaving the combined organisation have been treated well. This creates a greater degree of comfort and trust all round. One of the reasons for this is that even though they are staying they may think that they are 'next on the list'.

The rebuilding process has, at its core, the need for everyone to understand the reasons for the merger or acquisition and what the key measures of value will be in future. Not only do you need to protect the sources of value but you must begin to implement strategies to build on them as quickly as possible. The more that you communicate, the less people will make up their own minds for themselves. People will rapidly fill information vacuums - it is much better that you do this for them as it will be accurate and their confidence in the future will be significantly greater.

Chapter 12 - Restructuring delivers the goods

Managers must always tell the truth, with their actions matching their words. Even the appearance of a single falsehood will break confidence, erode trust and hinder short-term and long-term productivity.

Informing and responding to clients

Your customers should be viewed as one of the main stakeholders in a merger and treated as such. At the end of the day they generate your income. Customers have a degree of loyalty to a particular company or brand. If there was no customer loyalty at all then neither arm of the merging organisations would be successful. Therefore when companies merge, previous customers will decide for themselves whether to stick with the new company or to move elsewhere. Keeping them in the picture and explaining how they might or might not be affected is the best way of securing their future custom.

The benefits you have identified from having the larger merged organisation may not impress the customer because what they have valued has now been changed to something different. They may not see the merged organisation in the same way that you do.

You have to connect your people's activities with your customers' needs and you have to decide the extent to which you wish to build on existing customers versus creating a totally new client base. The levels of risk involved must be assessed as part of this process.

Systems

Remember whatever IT systems and other processes you have in both organisations, they will be backed up by a staff group familiar with the systems they have been working with. Merging these two groups is a people issue not just a technological issue. It should go without saying that a major part of aligning systems in merged companies is an issue about what you do with the staff, not just what you do with the technology. People are as important as the technology.

Chapter 12 - Restructuring delivers the goods

The approach we would promote is that, before the event, for the technology and systems to be looked at in parallel with the people who support them. An outline strategy needs to be determined to ensure that IT systems will fully support the newly merged organisation.

This must be followed up by an integrated programme of change for both the technology and the people involved in supporting it. This is likely to take a significant period of time. It is more important to get the right answer than a quick and sloppy answer.

> PriceWaterhouseCoopers surveyed senior executives from 125 companies worldwide to determine the biggest hurdles of M&A deals and found that integrating information systems is the toughest post-deal challenge. Nearly three out of four companies reported problems integrating information systems after a merger.

Summary

To increase the chances of success of mergers, acquisitions and restructuring the following steps are needed:

- The initial due diligence and collection gathering processes should be widened to assess the people involved and the 'softer' issues associated with the proposed change.
- A people strategy needs to be developed before pressing the implementation button so that, at that point, everyone understands how and when the issues relating to them personally will be dealt with.
- A programme of action needs to be undertaken to address the issue of merging different cultures involving as many people as appropriate from both organisations.
- The customer base of both organisations needs to be kept informed of changes as they happen and a feedback system should be created to enable them to comment about any concerns they may have.
- An outline strategy should be produced before the merger takes place of how to address the integration of IT systems and the people who operate them - this

Chapter 12 - Restructuring delivers the goods

should be followed by an implementation process to ensure the changes are effected in reality in the most effective way.

If two companies are intending to merge, or if departments are being restructured, and they have followed the steps outlined in this book there should be a high likelihood that the merger will be successful and that the new organisation will be a cohesive one.

Before turning to the final Chapter about 'how to do it' we relate in the next Chapter how the issues we have discussed thus far relate to the Public Sector in particular.

Chapter 13 - Cohesive Public Services

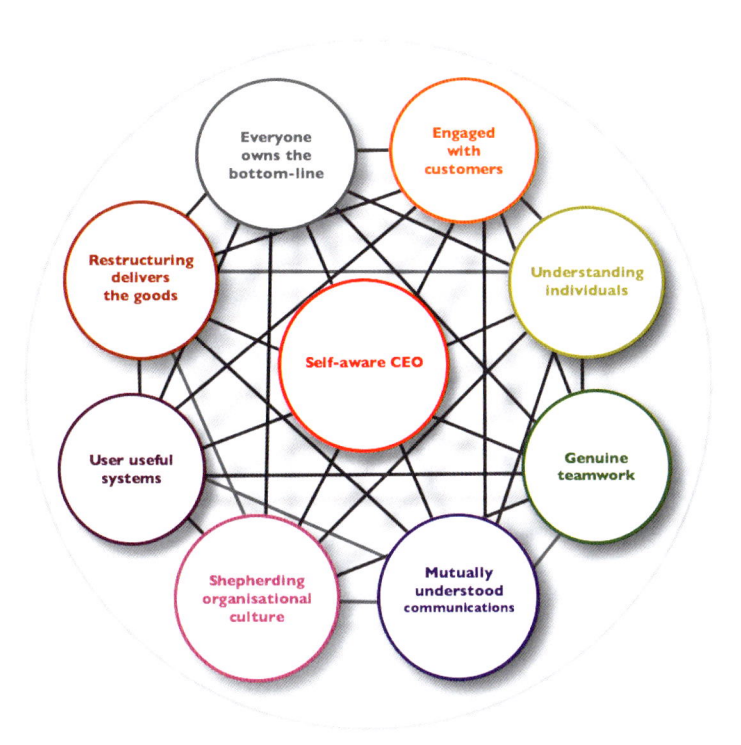

The Issue

Public sector organisations differ in certain ways from private sector ones. However they share many of the same issues. This chapter identifies differences and outlines how they relate to our holistic model. Some of the nuances may differ when applying the principles of cohesion to public sector organisations but the key issues are exactly the same.

Differences

The purpose of the Public Sector is to provide services to the public in an efficient and effective manner. It is not in the business of generating profits or expanding its range of influence and involvement except in meeting additional needs identified by the public. Whereas a private sector business can expand its range of products or services without asking anyone's permission, such changes in the public sector are normally effected as a

Chapter 13 - Cohesive Public Services

result of passing new legislation. Subtle changes can be made without such recourse and might result from different political emphasis or improved professional practice.

The second difference is the involvement of politicians in the decision making process. This has a tendency to make things less clear than might be the case in the private sector and certainly can make working relationships more complex.

Neither of these differences requires any fundamental change in our holistic model. The way in which cohesion may be achieved will have some differences but these are more ones of emphasis than substance.

Who should run public services?

In recent years there has been considerable debate in the UK as to who might provide public services most efficiently, the public sector or private businesses? Experience has shown that both sectors can potentially do this well and both can do it badly. The issue is more about the qualities, attitudes and approaches of the people running those services than about whether they are publicly or privately run.

In the private sector you need to make a profit. In the public sector you do not. The tendency is for the private sector to have greater flexibility than the public sector in what it does. If this flexibility is used to generate benefits in terms of effective services this is a good thing. If it is used merely to increase profits of the private sector organisation it may well not be.

One thing that should also be remembered is that replacing a large bureaucratic and inefficient organisation in the public sector with a large bureaucratic and inefficient one in the private sector may have no benefits whatsoever. Whilst the politicians involved may feel further away from taking any blame, the public who are receiving the services are getting no additional benefits. The focus should therefore be on who is providing the services, how they approach them and what results they deliver. Given the right people in the right places performing in the right way, success can be achieved in either sector.

Chapter 13 - Cohesive Public Services

The commonly accepted perception that the public sector is inefficient is no more true than the perception that all private sector businesses are run effectively.

If the process of choosing who runs a service is conducted by competitive tendering the tendency is to focus on comparisons of quantitative information. Great care needs to be taken in these circumstances that the qualitative information is not overlooked and that the quantitative is not accepted without question. It is all too easy for any organisation to write claims down on a piece of paper which are not subsequently delivered in practice. Direct evidence of track record and competence should be sought before making decisions as to who should run a particular service. Once a change is made to move to the private sector, returning such a service to the public sector will involve considerably more effort and cost.

When deciding whether to award tenders to one organisation or another the difficult part of the process concerns qualitative data, the ability to deliver the service properly. For example how do you judge whether a public or private sector organisation can deliver the necessary quality of care that you require for elderly or other vulnerable clients? They will have told you in the tender documentation what the prices and costs are. But can they deliver your required quality levels at these prices? It will be too late to take them to task after the contract has been awarded and they fail to deliver the requisite care. Vulnerable clients cannot have their time over again and may have had experiences that you would not want them to have. Tender documents, without the added element of qualitative checks and face to face contacts, are simply examples of bureaucratic box ticking.

Applying our holistic model to public services

Presented below are the differences of emphasis relating to each aspect of our model.

The self-aware CEO

In the public sector, the CEOs of government departments and local authorities are not in total command of everything to the same extent as their private sector peers. The reason for this is that there will be political discussions to which the CEO is not party, even though they may have provided advice beforehand. They then have to cope with implementing whatever is decided.

Chapter 13 - Cohesive Public Services

It is still of vital importance that the CEO is very self-aware of the impact of their own style. Like their private sector counterparts they have a connection to everything and an influence on all things. In a public sector context, CEOs need to have an understanding as to how their approach differs from or is similar to that of their political masters. Ensuring these combinations of politicians and officials are as positive as possible has the best chance of ensuring that the organisation performs effectively as a whole. The CEO needs to understand their personal style and approach (as measured by MBTI® and FIRO-B as described earlier) and manage it as effectively as possible. Nobody else is able to do that.

Everyone owns the bottom-line

As for the private sector it is just as vital, if not more so, that public sector staff have a clear bottom-line result that they own and seek to contribute to. The bottom-line is different in that it cannot be purely financially expressed except in that you are not supposed to exceed budgetary allocations. Bottom-line results are therefore qualitative in most respects notwithstanding the more recent use of numerical targets. Everyone needs to be sure of what the bottom line means in terms of the services they provide and in what way they are provided.

To do otherwise is to follow processes without understanding their purpose and without any heed to the consequences of not following them, or the implications of any judgement they may make. They become a substitute for focusing on the bottom-line.

The public sector is often characterised as following a series of processes. When things go wrong processes are called into question and revisions are made. If the same thing goes wrong again, further questions are asked and more revisions made. There is often a reluctance to talk about the result and why it occurred, and an avoidance of identifying who did and didn't to what.

For example if a child in local authority care unfortunately dies this clearly is not an acceptable result. Upon investigation it is often the case that staff involved are not subject to discipline or dismissal and the associated public enquiry focuses its recommendations on processes, not on individuals' responsibilities and whether they have been properly

Chapter 13 - Cohesive Public Services

carried out. It is easier to criticise processes than to deal with individual performance. This is not to say there should be a focus on blaming someone or finding a scapegoat. However as we have said earlier, it is people that generate results not processes. Therefore securing improved bottom line results must include how people perform.

Bottom-line results are short, medium and long term. Conflict between these needs to be managed effectively. Political outlook tends to be shorter term – will this decision influence my prospects of getting elected next time? Strategic issues such as infrastructure, energy, defence procurement, the impact of demographic changes, are longer term and do not fit in with a natural shorter term political timeframe.

Engaged with customers

The two groups of customers for the Public Sector are the direct customer of the service and the general public i.e. taxpayers. The former are looking for their specific needs to be met by the service in question whilst the latter are looking for overall effectiveness of delivery and its relationship with the cost of the service (affordability).

To some extent a parallel can be drawn with the customers of a private business and the company's shareholders who provide the necessary capital to run it. The difference between the public and private sector is that the public services have to be provided to everyone who is entitled to them, whereas in the private sector if you don't like one company's products you are free to switch to another.

Elected representatives may think that they represent customer opinion. However it is rare for customers of public sector services to be consistently and comprehensively consulted about their opinions of these services. The results of elections reflect many things but are not always a measure of the customers' opinions of specific services. Elected representatives therefore provide only a general view of public opinion and this may often only be the complaints not the positive comments. To get an accurate detailed picture, the public themselves need to be asked directly.

What most customers are really interested in is usually the detail of their specific interaction with the system e.g. can I get a hospital appointment, was I given the right

Chapter 13 - Cohesive Public Services

medicine, as opposed to whether or not the resources for the Health Service have been correctly distributed. It is possible therefore to ask the public for their opinions on specific issues in such a way that does not compromise the positions of their elected representatives. This would add valuable feedback information enabling the system to be adjusted in line with customers' needs.

There are a wide range of public services including regulatory functions and tax collecting. Asking customers' opinions about these particular kinds of services may not always elicit a positive reaction as a result e.g. someone whose premises has failed a public health inspection. However in every case customers should be able to give their opinions on how the service was delivered even if they may not have liked the result.

Understanding individuals

In the public sector all the points made in Chapter 7 are equally applicable as in the private sector.

A particular feature of the public sector is that it contains many people who are naturally attuned to following set processes. In layman's terms these are often referred to as bureaucrats. With these people, following systems consistently and reliably is a key strength. In a cohesive organisation they need to remember the underlying purpose behind what they are doing.

We have found a simple way of doing this is to ask first what the client or customer is trying to achieve, so that one can then say 'this is how you can achieve it in a way that is consistent with the governing rules and systems for that particular area'. If everyone were to begin with this question rather than assuming they know the answer an effective outcome is much more likely to arise.

There is a continuing need for managerial support, coaching, and training and development associated with making judgements and taking decisions attuned to the various public services sectors involved. There will often be no one right answer but a range of potential responses which could draw positive outcomes.

Many judgements have to be made without all the facts. The nature of the private sector means that people are attuned to this situation for business survival. In general terms you

Chapter 13 - Cohesive Public Services

will have more people in public sector organisations who are naturally attuned to operating with concrete facts than those who are happy to fill in the blanks of uncertainty. The ratio is likely to be at least 75:25. This reinforces an emphasis on process ahead of judgement and decision taking.

Genuine teamwork

All of the comments made in Chapter 8 on understanding teamwork apply in the public sector. The increasing need for government departments to work together, departments of local authorities and other agencies to work across organisational boundaries places a high premium on effectively melding the different cultures. In recent times in the UK the phrase 'joined up government' has been used. The public expect 'joined up government' as a matter of course. The reality is all too often disjointed as each part tries to look after its own patch. Concentration of effort is therefore likely to be required in this area.

Mutually understood communications

The complicating factor in the public sector in respect of communications is the conflicting perspectives and requirements of various stakeholder groups on any issue in question. This places a higher premium on having clear mutually understood communications. By following the model identified in Chapter 9 people will be more likely to be fully informed and to take into account one another's positions. This should optimise the likelihood of people supporting any final outcome.

Shepherding organisational culture

The purpose of shepherding culture is to continuously look to make 'the way we do things round here' better. The comments in Chapter 10 apply equally to the public as to the private sectors.

An additional issue in the public sector is the frequent use of inspection regimes to check that organisations are conforming to accepted standards.

Chapter 13 - Cohesive Public Services

Inspection is an overhead. You need to take hold of the inspection process so that it works for you and the continued development of your services not just for the needs of the inspectorate.

You should aim for parts to be inspected that you have a concern about, and you should ask for suggestions about what to do to improve those areas. It is no use for you to be told that you are doing something wrong in the absence of recommendations about how to put it right. You should also be checking on what basis the standards you are being checked against were arrived at and whether they have had any involvement and input from the customer.

You should also check that proper recognition is made for specific local circumstances which are different to what might be found in other areas of the country. Endeavour to ensure that inspections take opinions from customers. A school inspection will for example be more fully connected with its remit if it asks the pupils for their opinions.

In a wider context, it would make sense for standards of excellence to be set locally, involving the two principal groups of customers referred to earlier and using these as part of the inspection process. The day to day operations of the organisation need to be attuned to delivering against these local standards of excellence. You may not be in a position to design the national system for gathering data in a consistent way, but every senior manager should be capable of identifying what is critical locally for their organisation to deliver.

Inspectors should also be aware that their very presence directly affects what they are inspecting. They may not therefore gain a true view of what really happens unless they spend a long enough time in that particular organisation.

We also find that the practice of giving extra resources and freedom of decision making to organisations with an excellent performance rating is a practice that flies in the face of logic. It is tantamount to directing the international aid budget to the USA, Japan and Germany to the exclusion of impoverished third world countries. This surely is a nonsense. Organisations in the public sector should be encouraged to support moves to change things to a more sensible and improvement focused direction.

Chapter 13 - Cohesive Public Services

At the end of the day the question needs to be asked as to whether it is value for money to spend what is being spent on inspection as opposed to spending scarce resources and scarce people skills on the development of the organisations themselves. Ticking boxes adds nothing to front line services.

Previous comments made above about focusing efforts on processes versus focusing on results is an important part of the organisational culture.

User useful systems

Many systems in the public sector have a multiplicity of users. These include those carrying out operational functions, those managing them, and those who receive statistical information about that particular part of the organisation, whether locally, regionally or nationally. It is important to achieve the right kind of balance between these competing interests otherwise the day to day running of the system becomes an expensive overhead.

Restructuring delivers the goods

It is all too common in the public sector for reorganisations to be used as a means of addressing any and indeed every problem. It is an indication that something is being done even though the net result may not deliver the outcomes that customers and stakeholder might want. It is often a question in management consultancy speak of 'rearranging the deck chairs on the Titanic' than it is one of seriously addressing the real issues. It may be accompanied by insufficient investigation of what the real situation is as well as insufficient follow-through to generate actual required results on the ground. A great deal of time and effort and emotional energy can be devoted to such exercises – out of all proportion to the results. It would be better to identify more clearly the potential solutions for solving the identified problems in the first place than rushing headlong into these exercises.

No reorganisation should be undertaken unless it can be demonstrated to deliver significant improvements to the service. Its justification must begin with this and not be driven by purely internal considerations involving funding or the retention or the release of particular individuals. Reducing costs is not achieved by spending money on restructuring

Chapter 13 - Cohesive Public Services

which is an expensive exercise. No reorganisation should be undertaken without defining how the success of the exercise is to be measured and then measuring it.

Summary

There are many similarities between public and private sector organisations. Perhaps the key difference is a lack of clarity about what is the bottom line. Keeping this firmly fixed in everyone's mind will help the other parts of the cohesive jigsaw to fall into place.

Chapter 14 - How you do it

The Issue

If you wish to improve the cohesiveness of your organisation this chapter outlines how you might do it.

It is highly unlikely that any organisation can move from where it is now to a state of total cohesion in one step. The issue is therefore to identify what the steps are and in what order they should be taken to link the organisation together and improve bottom-line results.

Key steps of how to do it

We have identified 4 essential common sense steps that need to be taken to move towards a more cohesive organisation:

- Diagnosis - understanding where you are now and the steps that need to be taken to effect real change. This is as they are perceived in the current circumstances - events may change them over time.
- Programme - the means of starting the next step(s) towards cohesion.
- Coaching and mentoring – a means of reinforcing progress with individuals.
- Evaluation - understanding what progress has been made and how this affects future steps.

Diagnosis - what to look for

Diagnosis provides insights to ensure that efforts focus on the right things and on the order in which to do them to achieve real and lasting change. The types of things that it is important to know in making these decisions include:

- What you want to do with your organisation including organic growth, dividend growth, cost reduction, acquisition, mergers, sale.
- Your corporate strategy.
- Your people.
- Organisational effectiveness.
- What it is possible for your organisation to achieve.

Chapter 14 - How you do it

- Your perception of issues and problems.
- Your product/service set, market position and market share.
- The behaviour of your marketplace.
- Your financial results.
- Your future plans.
- Customers' and other stakeholder perceptions of you.
- Your use of resources including costs and waste.
- Your control and decision making structures.
- How your performance, behavioural and cultural standards are set and monitored.
- Organisational culture, rituals, behaviour and personality style.
- Staff attitude, alignment and teamwork.
- Your personal leadership and style.

The diagnosis is meant to be a clear and accurate snapshot of where the organisation is at present.

Programme

Based on the evaluation of the diagnosis, the next stage should be to develop a programme that addresses priority issues. The form that this takes will vary according to what needs to be done. They will usually consist of different forms of individual and group development, along with projects that are required to achieve desired end-results.

In terms of which places on the holistic model you might wish to start taking action, some are easier starting points than others.

- If you are reading this as the CEO, starting by being fully self-aware is a sound initial step. If you are not the CEO, "making" him or her self aware may not be the best starting point.

- Taking a team through Genuine Teamwork is an especially effective starting point as you should usually find one part of the organisation is willing to take it on board. This provides a springboard on which to build further teamwork and hence found a new organisational approach.

Chapter 14 - How you do it

- User Useful Systems can be addressed on a system by system basis and hence is another optional start point. Any changes though may take time to deliver.

- Understanding Individuals can be used to ensure that all future appointments, and promotions (and indeed performance and disciplinary issues) are dealt with effectively so that any problems which the organisation has are not being further compounded by inappropriate appointment decisions.

- The remaining elements all require some form of organisation wide application and may need to be fed through in stages. Changing what happens here will often usually not be achieved across the whole organisation in one single action programme.

Coaching and mentoring provides a practical hands-on way of reinforcing and building on the outcomes from more formal programmes and continues the development of managers involved. It is also an opportunity to reinforce the importance of seeking out the linkages and ensuring that these are addressed as well.

Evaluation

No programme should be undertaken without an evaluation of the progress and the results against your required outcomes.

Professional Support

We would recommend in following the above process you make use of some professional support at the diagnostic stage. This should ensure accurate assessment of where you are at the moment based on an independent viewpoint. It will provide a firm foundation on which future activity can be built.

In selecting who to use in this capacity it is important that you choose people who understand and have an affinity with the approach outlined in this book. They must also be people who can relate to you and to what the organisation needs to achieve and the way that you do it. The people you engage need to have a mixture of profiles to ensure that they tune in quickly to all aspects of your organisation.

You don't want to engage professional support that employs standardised solutions to problems, as these solutions may cause a whole series of extra problems in themselves.

Chapter 14 - How you do it

Whoever you use needs to demonstrate a proper understanding and commitment to the holistic approach outlined in this book.

Because of the nature of the diagnosis phase, the involvement of outside people who can ask the necessary awkward questions without fear or favour is needed. However you need to also use internal staff as the approach needs to be transferred into the organisation. It is particularly important to involve internal staff in designing and implementing the change programme that emerges.

Summary

Following the above approach should ensure that you achieve enhanced bottom line results for your organisation and build a sounder foundation for successful future performance. We wish you well in your endeavours to this end.

Missing Links Summary

Chapter 1   What is the problem?

A perfectly cohesive organisation is an ideal state to which all organisations should aspire. The focus should be on moving progressively towards it by taking actions which improve cohesion. Many things contribute to building this picture; we will be focusing in particular on:

- The organisation as a whole and the context within which it operates.
- Those specific elements which tend to be missed or generally not dealt with effectively.

The most effective treatment is for organisations to develop a state of mind and actions that opt for a holistic approach to the organisation and its challenges.

Over many years, in many organisations and in many countries the problem that we have frequently observed is that organisations do not work as a single integrated whole.

A wide variety of 'treatments' are offered to organisations. You need to focus in particular on:

- The organisation as a whole and the context within which it operates.
- Those specific elements which tend to be missed or generally not dealt with effectively.

Stated in a basic way, the most effective treatment is for organisations to develop a state of mind and actions that opt for a holistic approach to the organisation and its challenges.

Chapter 2   Myths and mistaken beliefs

The myths that help organisations to perform can also lead to mistaken beliefs that get in the way of performance improvement. The positive things you do can also have unforeseen negative consequences. The challenge is often to prevent your greatest strengths from becoming your greatest weaknesses.

Missing Links Summary

Chapter 3   Why our holistic approach?

The long term success of a business is centered on its ability to move in a controlled and effective manner from where it is to where it wants to be. It must focus and coordinate the energy of its actions and its people towards this goal in manageable sized steps. Following our holistic approach enables this achievement to take place.

Chapter 4   The self-aware CEO

The self aware CEO is an essential part of a cohesive organisation. This not only means knowing yourself but knowing the people you work with and the impact you have on them. Your effectiveness can only be achieved through what other people do. The way you lead will be an important determining factor in whether others follow.

Missing Links Summary

Chapter 5   Everyone owns the bottom-line

For an organisation to gain the maximum benefit from its potential everyone in it needs to share in ownership of the bottom-line. This bottom-line is not just the amount of profit the organisation makes but those other aspects that contribute to sustaining its health and success into the future.

Chapter 6   Engaged with customers

To engage with your customers you need:

- A differentiated product or service which can be presented as a consistent customer value proposition.

- You need to have consulted with and gained feedback from your customers.

- All parts of your business operation need to be aligned to supporting your customer proposition.

- Each person's actions need to be consistent with this.

Chapter 7   Understanding individuals

Your staff are truly your greatest asset. Without them you will not achieve any results. Getting the best from them will contribute greatly to realising your organisation's potential.

Chapter 8   Genuine teamwork

- Understand the contribution that each team member makes to the team and their individual personal style and approach.

- Understand the overall way in which the team approaches it's work.

- Understand the strengths, drawbacks and gaps within the team.

- Understand how each team relates to other teams.

Missing Links Summary

- Use that understanding wisely and proactively within and between team.

Chapter 9 Mutually understood communications

To provide effective communications you need to:

- Understand the 6 elements of effective communication as described in the Mobius model above.
- Follow these steps in the correct sequence.
- Pay particular attention to step 1 (establishing mutual understanding – not necessarily agreement).
- Irrespective of your personal style no-one is a fully effective communicator - this has to be continually worked on and feedback sought at every suitable opportunity.

Chapter 10 Shepherding organisational culture

The nature of your culture has a significant impact on the organisation's bottom-line. You need to shepherd it to ensure that this is a positive impact. The culture will not then get in the way of achieving business results.

Chapter 11 User useful systems

You should:

- Understand what your IT systems do.
- Ensure that computer generated information is not accepted without question.
- Ensure your IT Department/supplier and users work cooperatively together.
- Ensure your IT/supplier is involved in helping to move the organisation forward.

Missing Links Summary

Chapter 12   Restructuring delivers the goods

If two companies are intending to merge, or if departments are being restructured, and they have followed the steps outlined in this book there should be a high likelihood that the merger will be successful and that the new organisation will be a cohesive one.

Chapter 13 Cohesive Public Services

This Chapter summarise the aspects where the Public Sector is similar to or different from the Private Sector in respect of the issues dealt with in this book.

Chapter 14 How you do it

We have identified 4 essential common sense steps that need to be taken to move towards a more cohesive organisation:

- Diagnosis - understanding where you are now and the steps that need to be taken to effect real change. This is as they are perceived in the current circumstances - events may change them over time.
- Programme - the means of starting the next step towards cohesion.
- Coaching and mentoring – a means of reinforcing progress with individuals.
- Evaluation - understanding what progress has been made and how this effects future steps.

Phil Abbott graduated from Keele University and is a consultant and business psychologist with a main focus on organisational development, team building and change management. He has extensive practical experience in a wide variety of organisations in the public and private sectors.

Paul Fellows graduated from Oxford University and is a former MD in the financial-services sector with wide international experience in Europe, Japan and Australia. He specialises in business strategy, management development, change management, and marketing.

They are both results oriented and appreciate the multiple and interactive nature of challenges facing businesses and public sector organisations. They understand that fixing one element out of context can exacerbate rather than resolve the situation. Their diverse backgrounds in strategic and people management have been gained in the following sectors:-

- Local authorities
- Healthcare organisations
- Police authorities
- Probation services
- Government

- Financial services
- Insurance
- Banks and building societies

- Chemicals
- Textiles
- Glass manufacturing
- Food processing

- Tourism
- Transport
- Postal services

- Charities
- Higher education
- Career management consultancy

Notes